PRAISE FOR

If Rahab the Harlot Could, So Can You!

This book is a must-read for Christians from the spectrum of spiritual babyhood through spiritual adolescence to spiritual adulthood. You will find this book helpful in whatever stage of the spectrum of your spiritual growth. I pray that you will use this book as a good supplemental reading to the Bible.

Pastor Alexander Arthur, PhD
Word of Life Christian Center, Nashville, TN

The redeeming love of God comes through in so many ways in this book. Seeking Him, asking forgiveness, and speaking out what you want in your life are all so important. In such a time as this, the redeeming love of God is so needed. Jola's captivating style of writing kept me reading it all in one sitting.

Cherry Meadows
Vice President, Crown Enterprises

Wow. This amazing book by Attorney Jolade Olufon Moore is a masterful telling of God's faithfulness. This is a powerful testimony of how God can take someone who felt like they had messed up too much to be used by God and changed their circumstances. This is a great book, one that is certain to help you to live a fearless life, knowing that God is on your side and that His plans for you are good, not evil.

A. Deloris Alexander, Ph.D.
Tuskegee University, Tuskegee, AL

If Rahab the Harlot Could, So Can You is a compelling and motivational book that inspires hope and encourages change. This book is perfect for anyone seeking to overcome challenges, make empowered decisions, and live a life of purpose. Attorney Jola Moore's blend of biblical wisdom, personal testimony, and sage counsel makes this book not only a spiritual resource but a roadmap for personal transformation.

Barbara Ann Jeter
Eternal Heiress Ministries & Kings Hill, Board Chair

If Rahab the Harlot Could, So Can You is a beautiful testament to the expanse of Jesus's shepherding heart for us. Seeing how God spoke to Jola fuels our faith with testimony of a God who is moved by faith like a mustard seed and who makes all things right.

Will Hart
Chief Executive Officer, Iris Global

Once I started reading, I could not put the book down until I finished it. I see it as a tool for evangelism and a source of encouragement and inspiration for people who may think God does not exist. This book lets people know that He is a God who delights in the joy and prosperity of His people . I recommend this amazing and awesome book to everyone. My wife, Olufunmilayo (one of Jola's best friends from childhood) and I were one of the friends she visited to share the love of Jesus with after she met the Lord. We didn't understand what she was saying at the time, but she sowed a seed in our lives. We gave our lives to Jesus Christ not long after her visit. We are now serving Him as pastors in Lansing, Illinois.

Pastor Akintola Gbenro, M.D.
Household of Faith

If Rahab
the Harlot
COULD
So Can You

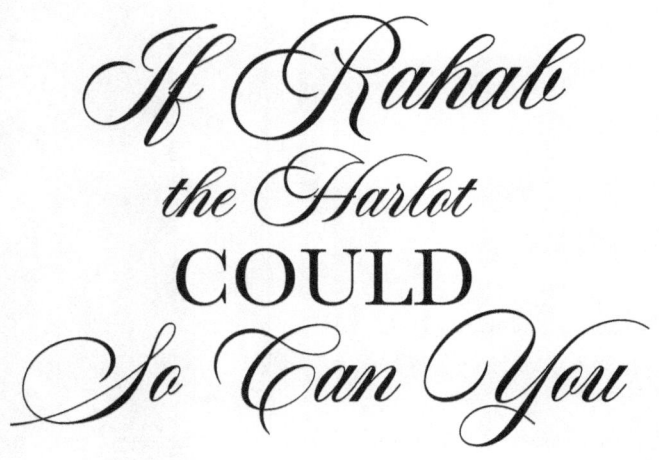

If Rahab
the Harlot
COULD
So Can You

A MEMOIR ABOUT THE POWER OF
DIVINE REDEMPTION

JOLA MOORE

For my parents, Gabriel Karunwi Olufon and Esther Adembipo Olufon, both of whom loved greatly and left a legacy of love, honor and unity.

For my parents-in-love, Bill & Dolores Moore, who loved and warmly welcomed my son and I into their hearts and family.

I thank God for you all and I believe, by faith, you are part of the cloud of witnesses, cheering us on.

Contents

Prologue

No, no, no! You know I can't do that! I can't accept that appointment! Obviously, they are mistaken! Obviously, they didn't hear correctly! They mean well and are some of the nicest, gentlest, most sincere people I have met. I believe they are sincere and have good intentions, but I am sure they are wrong!

How could they choose me? How could they go through this unique, pure process and still come up with the wrong answer? And how can they also be unanimous in that wrong answer? You know they are mistaken! You know all about me. You know how I broke my vow, cut corners, and fell flat on my face. You know I am not a good example or fitting role model for this group's young people, not after what happened to me!

You know I have no business standing up before any group to say anything worth hearing. You know I need to quietly sit in the back of the room, listen, and be taught. I am embarrassed at how I have ended up abandoned, rejected, and ashamed; I feel like I have let my family down, my friends down, and my church down. I let myself down, and most of all, I have let You down. Therefore, I certainly do not deserve any leadership role or position, nor am I worthy of it, *so you have to set them straight. You must correct them and tell them the type of person they really want to put in that position should be a pure, unspotted, and undefiled person who is deeply knowledgeable about You and will be a good role model for the young people. It should be someone who has not brought any shame to You and has not broken any vows to You. So, You have to tell them they are mistaken and that the choice for the leadership position simply cannot be me!"*

CHAPTER ONE

An Impassioned Monologue

That was my monologue with God during my Bible study time, also known as my "daily quiet time" with God early in the morning. Several seasoned believers, whom I looked up to and admired greatly and who had, in numerous ways, played a part in my epiphany, instructed me to start spending an hour of quiet time with the Lord every morning, preferably early in the morning. They had told me that was the way to grow in the Lord and develop an intimate and close relationship with Him.

They instructed me to start with prayer, move to praise and worship, read the Bible and then a Bible commentary, pray and talk to God, bring all my concerns to Him in prayer, and then listen for His answer. They said the answer might be immediate, or it may be later. However, I don't remember following all the steps on this fateful day! I was so distraught that I jumped straight to the "talking to God and bringing my concerns to Him" step. In fact, I was telling God all the reasons why the committee of elders was wrong and that He knows, like I know, that they were mistaken. And since they thought they had heard from Him, He would have to set them straight and help them correct their error.

After my long, impassioned monologue laced with tears, I finally quieted and stopped talking. Quietly, I waited for God to agree with me and assure me that He would set the committee of elders straight, show them that their decision was mistaken or misguided, and show them that the choice for the vacant assistant leader position for the Prayer Band could not possibly be me. I held my breath for several minutes, fully convinced that He would speak to me, agree with me, and fix the situation.

Then, I could continue to attend and enjoy the weekly Bible study sessions with my newfound spiritual family, the Prayer Band, and learn and be taught the word of God and His ways. I could continue to sit quietly in the back and learn more about this new joy, peace, and hope I have found without most of my newfound brethren knowing about my recent disappointment and rejection and how I had blamed God for it and said some mean things to Him. I just wanted to enjoy my restored, renewed relationship with God quietly and anonymously and keep my story to myself. I felt so sure that God would surely understand my position and agree, especially after my long and eloquent monologue succinctly stating my case and putting Him "in remembrance"!

CHAPTER TWO

God's Bewildering Response

After waiting quietly for what seemed like a long time but was probably just several minutes, God answered me! To this day, almost 40 years later, I cannot say whether it was an audible voice or a voice in my spirit. I can say unequivocally, without a shadow of a doubt, that God spoke to me, and I knew that it was Him even though, at the time, I did not understand His answer.

It certainly was not the answer I expected, but I knew it was God! His answer left me baffled and surprised; not only did He give me an answer I was not expecting, but He also did not agree with or respond to any of my stated facts, and worst of all, He did not explain His answer! I opened my eyes in bewilderment. What kind of answer is that? And what does that even mean?

God's answer that left me bewildered and speechless was this: *"If Rahab the Harlot could enter in, so can you."* I was dumbfounded and asked aloud, "Who in the world is Rahab the Harlot? Why am I being compared to a harlot? And where in the world did she enter into?"

Amazingly enough, although I was surprised and dumbfounded by the answer, I never once doubted or wondered if the answer had come from God. Strangely now, as I look back, I remember knowing without a shadow of a doubt that God had just spoken to me; He had just responded to my inquiry!

Even though I did not like or understand His response, and even though I had no clue what his response meant, nevertheless, I knew it was Him! The Most High God had just spoken to me!

How could I have been so sure that the response I heard had come from God? Why did I not consider that maybe it was just a thought in my mind, a figment of my imagination, or even the devil playing tricks on me in my troubled state of mind?

I could have questioned it more — mainly because I had never heard the voice of God like that before in my life. So, how could I be so sure? I didn't quite know the answer to that question, but the fact was, I did not ask those questions back then. They did not even cross my mind because I knew without any doubt that I had just received a response from God.

What makes this more intriguing is that I was still quite a "baby Christian," having just been "born again" less than one year before this incident occurred. I, therefore, had no prior experience to draw upon and no track record of prior conversations or encounters.

It was not until several years later that I began to understand why I had been so sure that it was God who had responded to me that day. As I studied the Bible, I discovered that John 10:27-28 (KJV) says, *"My sheep hear my voice, and I know them, and they follow me: and I give unto them eternal life; and they shall never perish, neither shall any man pluck them out of my hand."*

That explained it! I was one of His sheep, so I recognized His voice. I remember hearing a story of how shepherds led their flock of sheep by going ahead of them and either talking or singing, and the sheep would follow the sound of the shepherd's voice. It then made sense that when I consciously, as an act of my will, gave my life to Jesus and invited him to be Lord and master of my life, I became born again into His family. I became one of those "sheep" who know and hear His voice and follow Him.

I also read stories of several other people in the Bible who heard God speak and knew it was God, even though some had no prior experience hearing His voice. Some examples were Samuel and Saul.

Samuel was a young lad when he first heard the voice of God, so he thought it was Eli, the Chief Priest, calling out to him. Once he knew it was God, Samuel never again missed His voice. Then there was Saul. Saul had not heard the voice of God before the encounter on the road to Damascus when he fell off his horse, but he knew somehow that it was the voice of the Lord. Saul's life changed radically after that encounter, and he went on to write most of the New Testament. I instinctively knew what I heard from the Lord would mark the start of a significant shift in my Christian journey.

CHAPTER THREE

Who Is Rahab the Harlot?

I was sure it was God speaking to me, but I could not help but wonder: *Who in the world is Rahab the Harlot?* I had never heard of her, and why would God be talking about a harlot?

Without looking in the dictionary, I knew that harlots were not considered upright citizens or role models. I also know that harlot was another name for a prostitute, also called whores or ladies of the night. They were women who were promiscuous and/or sold their bodies for money or, to put it more succinctly, had sexual relations with men in exchange for money or material goods.

Why would the holy God talk to me about that kind of woman? What business could God have with a harlot, much less even mention one? As far as I knew, God could never have anything to do with such evil, vile people except to judge them and banish them to hell when they die, right? Surely, there are no harlots actually named in the Bible. Growing up reading the Bible and attending church, I had never heard of Rahab the Harlot. So, needless to say, after hearing this strange response from the Lord to my long monologue/prayer saying, *"If Rahab the Harlot could enter in, so can you,"* with no other explanation or instructions, no direct response on setting the elders straight, I was understandably perplexed.

I was so intrigued that I immediately got up off my knees, and my highest priority that day was to find out who this mysterious woman was that God had just referred to as "Rahab the Harlot" and why God was comparing me to her.

I must admit that I felt put down since God compared me to a harlot! I thought to myself *'Surely, I'm not that bad!* Nobody would ever dare compare me to a harlot; I am a university graduate with a professional degree and a bright, intelligent young lady from a good Christian family. I went to church regularly, sang in the choir, was baptized and confirmed in the church, and prayed from time to time.

Admittedly, I had slipped off the narrow path like many peers. I had gone further in a relationship than I had meant to, but surely, God understood and overlooked such mere human frailties!

We all justified our actions based on the same flimsy excuses like, "We are in love and in a steady dating relationship," or "We are in love and going to get married," or the mother of them all, "We are engaged, and so it's all right."

So, what if some of those relationships did not end up as we expected? Surely, then, God knew and understood that we are not perfect and that we would make those mistakes, didn't He? Just because I had "gotten caught," meaning I had become pregnant while we were engaged and then ended up breaking off the engagement and, therefore, having my child out of wedlock as an unwed mother, surely that does not qualify me to be compared to a harlot, does it?!

I did not sell my body; I did not have sexual relations in exchange for money or material goods, and I did not even have multiple partners, for crying out loud! I was engaged to the man I was in love with, and we thought that since we were now engaged and the wedding was still a while away, it was okay if we went a little farther than we had gone before. That could not have made me a harlot in God's eyes, or at least, I didn't think so. This pondering led me back to a single thought: *So, who was Rahab the Harlot?*

I had never heard of Rahab before that day. Not ever had I heard her name in a church sermon, a Sunday school class, the baptismal or confirmation classes I had attended at the Methodist Church, or the Methodist youth foundation camps and events I had attended all through my teenage years. Thus, she couldn't have been in the Bible. I mean, whoever heard of a harlot in the Bible? I thought maybe she was some historical figure, but then her name sounded sort of biblical, similar to other names I had read in the Bible, like the evil King Ahab.

I decided to look through my Bible concordance to see if I could find either the name Rahab or the word "harlot."

This event occurred in 1985, long before computers were fixtures in homes and before Google, Bing, or any other Internet searches were readily available. Research was done manually in books, at least by ordinary people.

I opened up my Bible, which had a very limited, small concordance in the back, and found neither the words "Rahab" nor "harlot." I thought, *I knew it couldn't be in the Bible! I knew it!* But then another thought came to my mind: *Then where else can it be?*

I knew without a shadow of a doubt that the answer I had heard came from God. I never doubted that fact, even though I did not understand the answer and it made no sense to me, but I thought that since God said it, it must be somewhere in the Bible! I then decided to get my father's giant Bible concordance, his treasury of Bible references, and his treasury of scripture references and do an exhaustive study to find out who Rahab the Harlot was and where she could be found in the pages of the Bible. As I plowed through this massive concordance and scripture reference manuals used by preachers and Bible scholars, I was soon awestruck and dumbfounded because there she was. I had found her!

Several Bible passages reference the name Rahab and the appendage the harlot, and then under "harlot," there she was again – the harlot, Rahab! She was referenced not once or twice but many times in the Bible! How come I had never heard of her?

I had been in church all my life and attended children's Sunday school and Bible studies at my church, but I had never heard of her. In addition, my father had started the tradition of family prayers every day since I was much younger. We would all gather together for family prayers, sing a song from our methodist hymnal, read a Bible passage, and then pray. I had never read about Rahab at our family devotionals either! But there she was, referenced in the treasury of scripture references and the Bible concordance: Rahab the Harlot!

CHAPTER FOUR

Traitor or Gambler?

I eagerly turned to the Bible passage, excited to read about this mystery woman God introduced me to! I was excited to find out who she was and her story since she was the reference point that God had used for me. How in the world did a harlot even get mentioned in the Bible not just once but several times? The biggest question for me was: *How did she go from being a harlot to becoming a role model, and where did she enter into? Was she an opportunist?* I turned to the first reference in Joshua 2 and began to read the amazing, incredible story of the woman known in the Bible simply as "Rahab the Harlot."

In Joshua 1, Moses, the great deliverer and leader of Israel, died, but God had ordained Joshua as his successor before his death. The Lord spoke to Joshua and instructed him to arise and go over the Jordan with all the people to the land He had given to them. Joshua then sent two men as spies and scouts to survey and view the walled city of Jericho. In Joshua 2, we read that the spies went to Jericho and came into Rahab's house and lodged there.

It was told the king of Jericho, Behold, there came men in here tonight of the Israelites to search out the country. And the king of Jericho sent to Rahab, saying, Bring forth the men who have come to you, who entered your house, for they have come to search out the land. But the woman had taken the two men and hidden them. So she said, Yes, two men came to me, but I did not know from where they had come. And at gate closing time, after dark, the men went out. Where they went I do not know. Pursue them quickly, for you will overtake them. But she had brought them up to the roof and hidden them under the stalks of flax which she had laid in order there. So the men pursued them to the Jordan as far as the fords. As soon as the pursuers had gone, the city's gate was shut.

JOSHUA 2:2-7 (AMP)

The Israeli spies had been spotted and identified as spies, and intelligence had informed the King of Jericho, who at once sent his officers to tell Rahab to hand the spies over. Rahab also had identified the men as Israeli spies as soon as they entered her establishment and had swung into action. She must have reasoned that the king's officers would have identified them as well and informed the king, who would undoubtedly have them apprehended. She at once decided to come to the aid of the spies.

Rabab took them up to the roof of her house and hid them under the stalks of flax that she had laid out to dry. By the time the king's men arrived at her establishment, she had already hidden the men. When they gave her the king's orders, she acknowledged that the men had come to her but had left just before the time to close the city gates, and she then urged the king's men to pursue the spies quickly. Why did Rahab align with the spies and betray her people? It is evident from the passage that Rahab immediately decided to help the spies when she saw them in her establishment and recognized that they were Israeli spies and not merchants or mere travelers from neighboring cities.

The normal response when you recognize enemies of yourself and your city, who you know mean you no good, would have been to sound the alarm or delay them there and send word to the King to send his soldiers to arrest them. But Rahab did not do that. She immediately took the men up to her roof to hide them. The other thing that she did not do was to bargain with them first. She did not make demands of them as a condition for her help; she just sprang into action and took the necessary steps to save them from being captured and most likely executed. As I read the story from Joshua 2, the big question in my mind was, *"Why?"* *Why would anyone, particularly a person of low estate like Rahab, take such an audacious action? Why would she betray her own people and side with the enemies? Why?*

I found the answers in Joshua 2: 8-13. Rahab stated unequivocally to the spies in Joshua 2:9 (KJV), *"I know that the LORD has given you the land."* How did she know that? She stated further that the terror and fear of the Israelis had fallen upon all the inhabitants of Jericho and that they were in despair because of Israel. Then she revealed how she knew, in Joshua 2:10 (AMP), stating, *"For we have heard how the Lord dried up the water of the Red Sea for you when you came out of Egypt, and what you did to the two kings of the*

Amorites who were on the [east] side of the Jordan, Sihon and Og, whom you utterly destroyed."

It would make sense that many travelers or artisan sojourners, merchants, tradesmen, and salesmen would come through the type of establishment run by Rahab. It would have been a type of tavern, salon, or Madam's house where there would be wine and women available for the sojourners and, if needed, maybe even overnight lodging.

Her establishment was on the city wall, probably close to the city gates, the entrance into the city. The men, the customers to the tavern, would sit around to eat or drink and relax from their journey and would naturally exchange stories of the experiences they had seen or heard as they traveled. As the owner and Madam of the establishment, Rahab was likely the one to welcome the customers and ensure they were served and comfortable. She would interact with them and learn more about them, their journeys, and their experiences. As the Madam and chief hostess of the tavern, she would have highly developed people skills just from her daily and constant contact with people from various countries and cultures.

In addition to the travelers and sojourners, most likely, the leaders and men in authority in Jericho would have been regular guests and customers at her tavern as well. Even the king of Jericho knew who Rahab the Harlot was, for he sent word personally to her through his officers and even explained why he was asking her to turn the men over to him. Some historians suggest that Rahab may have been a former concubine of the king, who was smart enough after her time as the king's concubine came to an end, to negotiate for herself a choice piece of property in the city of Jericho to start her own business of running a tavern or saloon and thereby become an independent woman, not needing to be kept by any other man.

We know from the story of Abraham and Sarah, his wife, in the Bible that kings at that time had the power to "take" any woman they fancied to become one of their concubines. The king at that time, having been told that Sarah was Abraham's sister, had sent his officers to take her and bring her to his palace to become one of his concubines. Abraham had lied and asked her to lie also and tell people she was his sister because she was a very beautiful woman, and Abraham was afraid that some men would kill him just to take her from him. We read in that story of how God himself stepped in to save Sarah from being violated by the king and had her restored back to Abraham, her husband. But this story not only shows us the power of the kings of those times but also how powerless women were and how they had no say in determining their lives and futures.

The historians suggest that Rahab was likely a beautiful young lady from a common family whom the king had taken to be part of his harem. She had no choice in the matter and no options. After being a king's concubine, a woman's chances of becoming married and respectable would have dwindled to zero. So, it appears that Rahab, being a highly intelligent young lady, decided to use her influence while she was still a favored concubine, and before the king would predictably tire of her and move on to the next beautiful concubine, she convinced him to give her a house on the wall and allow her to run a tavern or an inn so she could fend for herself and her family. It is easy to discern Rahab's intelligence and leadership skills in how quickly she decided to aid the spies and how quickly she acted once she made the decision.

One of the characteristics of great leaders is their ability to recognize great opportunities and immediately act on them. Opportunity is defined as a time or set of circumstances that makes it possible to do something, or, as someone else quaintly put it, "luck is when opportunity meets preparedness." Rahab immediately recognized the Israelis for who they were, as did some other citizens of Jericho. She immediately determined that she would help the spies by hiding them before the king's officers inevitably came looking for them to arrest them; otherwise, she would forever lose the opportunity to help them.

Someone else very aptly stated, "The opportunity of a lifetime is only good for the lifetime of the opportunity." Rahab the Harlot obviously understood that principle since she immediately sprang into action once she recognized the opportunity presented to her. Once she had led the two men onto the roof of her house and hidden them under the stalks of flax laid in order upon the roof, she immediately went back down to the tavern and was ready to receive the king's men who came in hot pursuit to arrest the Israeli spies.

The other pointer to Rahab's high intelligence is that she did not deny that the men had come into her tavern, for to do so would have raised suspicion about her truthfulness because other people saw them come in and recognized that they were spies.

Instead, Rahab agreed with the king's men and admitted that the men had come into her tavern but that she did not know where they had come from. She then told them that the men had gone out just before the time of shutting the gate when it was dark, but she did not know where they had gone. She painted a picture for the soldiers, showing that the spies had probably slipped out through the gates of Jericho under the cover of darkness just before the city gates were shut.

The story sounded true and plausible; in fact, it made sense that the spies would have used the cover of darkness to escape, having gathered the information they needed. She then urged the king's men to pursue the spies quickly, assuring them that they would overtake and apprehend them. She was clearly credible, convincing, and authoritative because the soldiers, without hesitation, acted on her suggestion and took off pursuing the spies outside the city wall towards the Jordan River.

CHAPTER FIVE

When Opportunity Meets Preparation

The amazing fact about Rahab that first exemplified her unusually high intellect, sense of discernment, and masterful negotiating skills was that she did not negotiate with the spies before helping them. She did not ask them for anything beforehand; she simply sprang into action and assumed the risk of lying to the soldiers and sending them on a wild goose chase. If the soldiers had not believed her and had searched her tavern and found the hidden spies, she would have been arrested along with the spies and possibly tried for treason and lost her life.

By not making any prior demands or placing any conditions on her assistance and by first risking her life on their behalf, Rahab won their trust, admiration, and gratitude. She was able to write her own freedom ticket to ask for everything she wanted.

The city gates were shut after the king's men had gone off on their wild goose chase after the spies. Then Rahab came up to the Israeli spies to explain to them why she had risked her life to protect and save their lives and why she had chosen to betray her own people and throw herself at the mercy of the Israelites. She recounted to them all that she had heard about their God and the exploits He had performed on their behalf.

However, her first statement explains why Rahab betrayed her people and helped the Israeli spies. She stated emphatically in Joshua 2:9 (NKJV), *"I know that the LORD has given you the land,"* and not "I have heard or suspect." That knowledge guided and dictated her subsequent actions — the NKJV version of the Bible states it even more succinctly. She told the spies, *"I know that the Lord has given you the land, that the terror of you has fallen on us, and that all the inhabitants of the land are fainthearted because of you* [Joshua 2:9 (NKJV)]." Webster defined "know" as being *"in possession of exclusive knowledge or information, broadly well informed."*

Rahab gives them the intel they had come to gather, that the people of Jericho had heard of all the exploits of the Israelis, all the victories their God had won for them, the kings and cities that had been utterly destroyed on their behalf, and that the people of Jericho had completely lost courage and fear had gripped their hearts. They had, in effect, already given up in their minds and were living in fear, waiting for the time when the actual defeat and overthrow would occur. They were, however, still going to put up a fight, hide behind their Great Wall, and see if they could fool the Israelites with their show of strength. However, Rahab had gone one step further than just hearing and believing the stories of the conquests and remarkable miraculous exploits of the Israelites. She had come to recognize that the secret of the Israelites was not their might or prowess but that the secret of their outstanding and miraculous victories was their God, and she had made up her mind to throw herself on his mercy. She had concluded that the God of Israel is the real deal, that he is God. In Joshua 2:11b (NKJV), she states unequivocally, *"For the LORD your God, He is God in heaven above and on earth beneath."*

After declaring her belief in their God and letting them know that she knows the real source of their power, Rahab then makes her demands, not just to them, but she demands that their God be the central, essential part of the agreement. She had obviously done her homework and knew the custom of the Israelis was to handle important commitments and promises through an oath and that when they swore by their God, they could not break it. She also knew enough to ask them for a tangible token to prove their agreement.

This incident brings to mind other times when other Israelis had used oaths and symbols to seal important agreements. Tamar had asked Judah for a pledge of his promise to give her a young goat from his flock in exchange for being intimate with her. He agreed to pledge his seal and cord and staff [Ref. Gen.38:16-18]. Also, the closer kinsman redeemer gave Boaz his sandal as a token of his agreement that Boaz should redeem and marry Ruth in his stead, in accordance with the custom in Israel concerning redeeming and exchanging property [Ref. Ruth 4:7-8].

However, these were customs peculiar to and practiced only by the Israelites. Yet, somehow, Rahab had researched the Israelites and their God to the point that she knew their customs on how to confirm transactions. She had become a secret admirer of their God, so much so that when the opportunity presented itself for her to change her allegiance from the idols of her people and throw herself on the mercy of this great God whom she had come to admire so much, she immediately sprang into action without hesitation or further thought.

The other interesting fact about Rahab the Harlot was her amazing negotiating skills, such as her ability to drive a hard bargain. She did not just ask for her own life to be spared when the Israelites conquered Jericho. No! She asked that they save the lives of her father, her mother, her brothers, her sisters, and all that they had, including their families and their possessions. She drove a hard bargain to include her entire family, but she only made her demands after she had saved the lives of the spies, shown them kindness, and let them know that she was an admirer of their God. She had rightly figured that they would be men of honor and would reciprocate her kindness and honor any pledge made in the name of their God.

CHAPTER SIX

The Scarlet Cord in the Window

What is the significance of the scarlet cord in the window? Joshua 2:15 states that Rahab let the spies down by a cord through the window for her house was upon the town wall. Then, in Joshua 2:18 (KJV), the spies instruct Rahab on how to save her and her family as agreed. They instructed her to *"bind this line of scarlet thread in the window which thou didst let us down by."* The spies instructed Rahab to bind the same scarlet cord or thread she had used to lower them down from the window. She was to leave that scarlet thread or cord tied in the same window from which she had let them down.

Rahab would not have known the significance of a scarlet cord, nor could she have pre-planned to let the spies down specifically with a scarlet-colored cord or thread. I believe that God supernaturally ordained it, that she chose the scarlet cord to let the Israeli spies down from the window without realizing or understanding the significance of the scarlet cord.

Several years before the Israelites arrived at Jericho, while they were still slaves in Egypt, God had instructed them to mark the entrance of their homes, their doors or mantels with the blood of the lamb they had been instructed to kill. Every Israelite who obeyed by marking their front door or mantel with blood, the Angel of Death passed over their household, sparing the life of their firstborn son. In contrast, none of the Egyptian homes had the mark of the blood on their front door or mantel, so their firstborn sons were all killed that night by the Angel of Death, including the Pharaoh's son.

The scarlet blood on the front door mantel was the divinely appointed sign that God used to save the Israeli firstborn sons. Now, the scarlet cord utilized in the spies' escape is also being used as the sign to spare the lives of Rahab and her entire family, whom she would have gathered into her house before the Israelites conquered Jericho.

Could Rahab have heard the story of the Angel of Death and the blood on the doorpost and deliberately picked out a scarlet cord to save the spies by letting them down through her window?

That could not be remotely possible given the facts of the story: the mission was top secret, the appearance of the spies at Rahab's salon was unplanned and unexpected, and all the actions that Rahab took had to have been quick and spontaneous. It would be reasonable to conclude that she did not have time to plan or decide on the color of the cord used for escape, which means the scarlet cord was God-ordained and not a coincidence. God divinely arranged that the cord she chose to let the spies down from the window to safety was scarlet, like the color of the blood the Israelites had used to put on their mantels and doorposts to save the lives of their firstborn sons on the night the Angel of Death visited Egypt. It was also the same color as the blood shed for our salvation on Calvary's cross thousands of years later.

The scarlet cord was how Rahab saved the spies' lives by lowering them from her window on the wall to safety. Thus, Rahab had her proof of their agreement; the scarlet cord also became the symbol by which the spies saved the lives of Rahab the Harlot and her entire family. With the cord left hanging from her window, she had to then gather her father, mother, brethren, and all her father's household into her house. Thus, whosoever should go out of Rahab's house, marked by the scarlet thread or cord, would lose his life, and his blood would be upon his head.

Everyone in the house with Rahab was covered by the covenant sealed by the scarlet thread. Rahab and her entire family came under the protection of the blood, symbolized by the scarlet thread in the window that made all the soldiers of the Israeli army "pass over" that one house on the city wall and destroy everyone and everything else in the entire city of Jericho.

Rahab the Harlot and her entire family became the sole survivors of the battle of Jericho because a harlot chose to put her trust in the God of Jacob and to cut a covenant with him. Rahab made it clear to the spies from the beginning that her decision to risk her life to save theirs was not because of them but because of their God. She declared in Joshua 2:11 (ASV), *"For Jehovah your God, He is God in the heavens above, and on earth beneath."* She demanded an oath by Jehovah their God that they would spare herself, her father, mother, brethren, and sisters and all that belonged to them and deliver their souls from death.

The Israeli spies recognized that the oath was not just between them and Rahab but between Jehovah, them, and Rahab. The spies made it clear when they told her in Joshua 2:17-19 (KJV), *"We will be blameless of this thine oath which thou hast made us swear,"* if she and her entire family did not precisely follow the instructions they had given her. Rahab knew that because their God was involved in the covenant, they could not back out of it or renege on it as long as she kept her side of the bargain and followed their instructions.

CHAPTER SEVEN

The Audacious Heroine

Finally, I knew who Rahab the Harlot was. I found that she was a very intelligent, audacious, and spontaneous woman who knew how to negotiate, could drive a hard bargain, and had a lot of insight, discernment, and wisdom. I also knew that it would be a mistake to write off or overlook this mighty woman because of her past and the title the world had put on her. The fact was only she and her entire family survived the battle of Jericho. All the other inhabitants of Jericho, including their king and nobles, all perished, and the whole city was destroyed.

It is obvious that the classification that society put on Rahab the Harlot as a low-life, lower-class, dumb woman of leisure, one who sold her body for money and favors, unintelligent, and certainly not one to be reckoned with or esteemed, was highly and terribly wrong. She had proved herself the most intelligent and wisest woman in Jericho and lived to prove it while also saving the lives of her entire family.

But, I could not help but wonder, what did Rahab the Harlot have to do with me regarding God's answer to my plea? I still did not fully comprehend God's answer to me in my distress when He said, *"If Rahab the Harlot could enter in, so can you."*

Now I know who Rahab was, but where did she enter into? Was it into the promised land with the Israelites after the battle of Jericho? Or was it into becoming part of the covenant of God with Israel because she had put her trust in him? Did she, like Ruth the Moabites, who told her Israeli mother-in-law, "Your God shall be my God," also become one of God's people because of her beliefs and actions? I decided to search the Bible to see if Rahab the Harlot was mentioned anywhere else outside the book of Joshua.

What I discovered blew me away and left me speechless. When I saw the other places where Rahab the Harlot was mentioned in the Bible, my jaw dropped in awe, amazement, respect, and admiration for this mighty woman, Rahab the Harlot! When I saw where she had entered, I understood what a high compliment the Lord had paid me by comparing me to her when He said, *"If Rahab the Harlot could enter in, so can you."* Rahab the Harlot had entered into the most exclusive and royal bloodline on the face of the earth. The highest, most prestigious, most revered family line in the whole world, and Rahab the Harlot was able to "enter in" to become a member of that family.

CHAPTER EIGHT

How Did I Get Here?

L et me back up to what had happened in my life that led me to this place. I was born in Warri, Nigeria. My father was a produce manager and moved around the country because of his job. But most of my childhood recollections were in Lagos, Nigeria, where we lived from my early childhood into my adulthood. Even though my family was Methodists, most of us kids attended Catholic schools.

At that time, the Catholics were reputed to run the best schools in the country. They had strict rules, regulations, and guidelines, as well as very pretty school uniforms that all the students had to wear to school every day. I still fondly remember my blue and white uniform consisting of a white short-sleeved cotton shirt with a knee-length sleeveless pinafore dress worn over the shirt. The pinafore dress had one large pleat in front and one large pleat at the back. We used stiff starch on the cotton pinafore to iron the large pleats to stand out and be crisp. The nuns, who were our teachers, would inspect our uniforms on Mondays at the school assembly to ensure all our uniforms were clean, crisp, and well-ironed. After passing inspection and the assembly concluded, we would march off to our classes by twos in our clean, crisp, well-ironed uniforms.

I have happy memories of my primary and secondary school years at the all-girls school, Our Lady of Apostles. The only setback was that I graduated with higher grades in my art subjects and low grades in my sciences. This occurrence was a setback because my father wanted me to go to medical school and had convinced me that an intelligent young lady like me should be a doctor and that I was so smart that I could excel in any subject, including all the sciences, if I put my mind to it.

So, because I loved my father very much and wanted to please him and wanted him to be proud of me, I agreed to attend the Federal School of Arts and Science in Victoria Island, Lagos, Nigeria, for one year to take remedial courses in physics, chemistry, and biology. There, I would retake the Ordinary Level exams in those subjects to raise my grades to As and Bs and increase my chances of getting admission into medical school.

I agreed to this plan even though I did not really like or enjoy physics, chemistry, or biology, and I did not have a natural aptitude for them as I had for literature, English, history, and drama. I figured that, as my father said, I just needed to put my mind to it, focus, and study harder, and surely a smart girl like me could raise those physics, chemistry, and biology grades to A's and B's. Everything was going smoothly for the first six months as the lectures were reviews of all the courses. After the halfway point of this one-year remedial course, they started to give us quizzes and tests in all the courses every week!

That was when the panic set in because I was not doing well in those quizzes and tests, especially in physics and chemistry. It did not matter how hard I studied or how many times I went over the materials; I was barely passing the class, and I was far from the A & B grades I had hoped to get.

Some of my new friends and classmates invited me to join a study group, suggesting that it would help me study and prepare better for the quizzes and tests. I eagerly agreed, thinking this was the missing piece. Studying with other science students who were much stronger and smarter than me would help me study better, understand and retain more, and thereby raise my test scores.

I attended several study groups, listened to the discussions, and watched as the same two or three students in the group would always show the other students how to solve the problem and analyze how they arrived at the correct answers. I saw how effortlessly these students would explain complicated science principles to the rest of us and arrive at the correct answers easily. After attending several of these study sessions, I began to doubt how smart I really was; next to these genius classmates, I felt like an outright dummy!

I began to develop an inferiority complex and would not open my mouth at the study sessions for fear that the other students would find out just how little I knew!

I began to despair as it became apparent to me that no matter how hard I studied, I could never have the knowledge and aptitude of these genius classmates to understand those complicated science principles or solve those mind-numbing science problems. Forget about having their aptitude! I was terrified that I would not even pass the classes, much less obtain an A or B grade, thereby disappointing my father again by dashing his hopes of me going to medical school to become the doctor in the family.

CHAPTER NINE

My Epiphany

The Merriam-Webster dictionary defines epiphany as *"a moment of sudden revelation or insight."* The word is further described as an "aha" moment when a person is suddenly struck with a life-changing realization that changes the rest of their story. It usually begins with a small everyday occurrence or experience.

I had my epiphany, my sudden revelation, during one of the study sessions at the Federal School of Arts and Science. The more I attended the study sessions, the more my despair increased about my ability to pass the course or improve my grades. The truth of the matter was that while I was still struggling to grasp and understand some science principle or formula, the group had moved on to another principle or chapter, so I was falling behind both in the study group assignments and the class assignments.

I began to feel overwhelmed, desperate, and scared. The desperation and fear brought about feelings of depression and hopelessness, which exacerbated my feelings of inferiority. I felt so out of my league with all these science whiz-kids, like an upstart, a fraud, a wannabe. I felt like I did not have what it took to be at that institution and, therefore, should not be there, and I walked around scared that I would soon be discovered as an impostor and put out or flunk out.

On this day, I attended the student study group and sat there wondering what I was doing there and why I had come back. The group was so far ahead that I did not even really know or understand what they were talking about or discussing. I was too scared and embarrassed to ask any questions since it would make it obvious just how far behind I was and how little I understood. I decided before the group was over that I would not come back or attend another study group. It was clearly not doing me any good, and I had fallen so hopelessly behind in the study assignments that the discussions were all above my head.

As we were about to leave at the end of what I had decided would be my last study session with the group, the student who had led the discussion group that night, one of the whiz-kid science geeks who explained the complicated science problems to the rest of the group, came up to me and what he said to me caused my epiphany, my moment of sudden revelation and insight.

I had looked at this guy with awe and wonder like he walked on water because of his obvious grasp of complicated science theories and the ease with which he explained the theories to the rest of us and solved science equations that still left me baffled even after he explained and solved them. I had also heard from other students that he was there to raise his B+ grades in two of the sciences to A+ to increase his odds of getting admission to the premier medical schools.

I thought, what an overachiever; it's brainiacs like him that make the rest of us feel inferior and unworthy! So, I avoided him and never went up after study sessions like other students to talk or ask for clarification. It was obvious to me that we were not in the same stratosphere academically, so I would not humiliate myself by opening my mouth and letting everybody else find out.

On the day that I decided not to come back or waste any more time at the study sessions but would spend the time catching up on my backlog of assignments, the whiz-kid walked up to my friend and me and asked my friend while looking directly at me, if this was the person she had told him about. I looked at my friend with a puzzled look, wondering what whiz-kid was talking about; ignoring me, she promptly said yes and introduced me. Whiz-kid greeted me as he reached out his hand and said, "I heard you got an A grade in English and would like you to help me raise my D grade in English to at least a B so that I can meet the requirements for the premier medical school's admission."

That was the moment I had my epiphany! I stood there in shock and disbelief at what I had just heard; that brainiac whiz-kid had failed a subject in which I had always excelled, and he was asking little ole inferior me for help to pass that subject! So, contrary to what my father had told me, not everybody who was smart excelled in English and literature or could even pass it!

It was like the sun and moon aligned that day as fireworks went off in my head; the depression and inferiority complex lifted right off my shoulders, my back straightened up, and I held my head up high. I felt like singing, "The Hills Are Alive," like Maria from the movie *Sound of Music!* The realization hit me like a ton of bricks as I figured out I was also a brainiac and a whiz-kid in another arena, and in that arena, I excelled and was looked up to by others.

That was the day I decided that I did not have the desire nor the requisite academic skills to go to medical school; in addition, I did not even like the smell of hospitals or being in one. The only thing I found attractive about becoming a doctor was the title, the prestige, and the money I heard they made.

I decided that day that as much as I loved my father and wanted to please him, I was never going to be a medical doctor, and I was going to return to the arena in which I was a whiz-kid and explore my options. In the meantime, since I had already paid and registered for the remedial exams, I would sit for them but decided that this would be the last time I sit for any exams in the science field.

CHAPTER TEN

How Do I Tell My Father?

I t is hard to describe how I felt in those ensuing days, the lightheaded, giddy feeling that I was not inferior to my peers. I was not a dummy or a dunce, but I was, in fact, quite accomplished in a different field. The feeling was so freeing and euphoric. The understanding that just because you are intelligent does not mean that you can excel in every field. For the first time in my life, I understood that we each had a natural gift or talent God gave us. In the area of our gift or talent, we excel almost effortlessly or at least with less effort than those not equally as gifted in that area or field.

The only dent in my newfound euphoric freedom was how to tell my father that I was going to totally abandon the science field and walk away from his dream of me becoming a medical doctor. Even though I loved that my father thought I was so smart and brilliant and could excel in every field and was so proud of me, I knew it was time to tell him the truth and lay that dream to rest. I had no idea where to go from where I was or how to get there, and I certainly did not know how to break the news to my father. I decided to wait until the results of the exams were released, and predictably, I did not do too well. I raised my grade to a B+ in biology but maintained the same grade in physics and chemistry. I shared the grades with my parents, thinking that even though my father would be disappointed, surely he would now realize that the sciences and medicine were not my calling or natural bent.

On the contrary, my father decided that with a little more focus and determination, I could raise my grade in the other two subjects if I went back to the school of science for another year and retook physics and chemistry. I was dumbfounded and tried to argue, but my father would not take "no" for an answer and insisted that I register for another year.

With that, all the fears, doubts, and insecurities came rushing back at the thought of returning to the science school for another year. I appealed to my mother to intervene on my behalf, but my lack of other options or other avenues made that difficult. My father said that if I would just put all my mind and heart into it, focus, and persevere for just one more year, I would succeed.

Even though I now knew better after my epiphany, I could not convince my father or shake his conviction that if I put my "brilliant mind" to anything, I could succeed. He was determined. As proof, he cited the fact that I had raised my scores in one subject and could do the same for the other two subjects if I persevered and put my mind to it. With sadness and a heavy heart, I returned to register for another year at the school of science in obedience to my father; that was when God intervened on my behalf!

At the Federal School of Arts and Science, I ran into my old English teacher and Vice Principal of my secondary school, Our Lady of Apostles, Mrs. Sosan, at the registration desk. She was surprised to see me and asked me why I was there. When I explained that I was registering for another year to raise my science scores, she was dumbfounded as she exclaimed loudly, "You are not a science student!"

She went on to remind me that I had been her best student both in English and Literature and had won a school award for writing an original drama piece for my class to perform for the end-of-year PTA competitions. She reminded me further that my class had won the prize for best performance, and I had also won the prize for the best actress in the leading role in the play.

Mrs. Sosan remembered that I had not shown much aptitude for the sciences and wanted to know why I would pursue the sciences rather than the arts, at which I excelled. She was horrified when I confessed to her that it was not my choice but that I was doing it at my father's insistence so I could go to medical school. She sent me home with an appointment for my mother and I to meet with her the next day at her office.

It turned out she was now the principal of Methodist Girls' High School, and they offered a two-year Higher School Certificate program equivalent to a baccalaureate or Community College degree and required for admission to most universities in Nigeria. At the meeting at her office, she reminded my mother of my strength in the arts and informed her that I had no business enrolling in a school of sciences.

Mrs. Sosan promptly offered me admission into Methodist Girls' High School's Higher School Certificate program to study English, Literature, and Government/ Political Science. I was jubilant, excited, and incredulous at my change in fortune. I excitedly accepted the admission offer with my mother's blessing and her assurance to Mrs. Sosan that she would break the news to my father. I happily packed my belongings and headed off to Methodist Girls' High School for the two-year Higher School Certificate program and my first boarding school experience.

This was my first experience moving away from home into a girl's boarding school. Even more, I was moving away thanks to a principal who thought highly of me, stood up for me, and opened the door for me to study subjects I loved and excelled at. This time, I wanted to bust out singing, "I can see clearly now; the rain is gone!" Truly gone were the cloudy days of feeling inferior, feeling like a dunce, and struggling with all the science subjects I could not seem to understand. It was finally going to be a bright, *sunshiny* future.

CHAPTER ELEVEN

Studying the Arts & Law

I have great memories of my time at the Methodist Girls' High School, meeting and making great new friends, enjoying my classes, and signing up for several afterschool activities. I acted in several plays and reveled in my newfound freedom to choose my subjects and activities. It was truly a freeing experience!

Being in a boarding school for the first time in my life, after my challenging year at the Federal School of Arts and Science, felt like going away to finishing school. I had finally shaken this burden that I was my father's last hope for a medical doctor from among his ten children and that I was letting him down and breaking his heart by not continuing along the difficult (to me, impossible) road to becoming a medical doctor. Being in boarding school meant that I didn't have to see my father till the end of the semester, and the schools closed for the Christmas holidays. By then, I would have been gone for several months, and the yuletide, happy season helped overshadow any lingering hurt or disappointment.

At the end of my two years at the Methodist Girls' High School, I was admitted to the University of Lagos, Nigeria, to study English and Literature. This three-year course would earn me a bachelor's degree. My father encouraged me to consider switching to a professional track during my first year. His philosophy was that we, his children, should strive to pursue professional courses that would enable us to become self-employed and "hang out our own shingle" if we so desired in the future. He felt that we should not put ourselves in a position where we would always need to be employed by a third party or company.

With the encouragement of my father and my older brother Gbolahan, who had then graduated from the Faculty of Law, University of Lagos and was practicing as a lawyer with the government, I switched my major from English and literature to law and started as a first-year law student in the Faculty of Law. My father was excited for me; he felt that if I could or would not become a medical doctor, then becoming a lawyer was a respectable and acceptable second choice!

My dating life at the university was not so memorable. I just never seemed to meet the "right person." I dated a few "acceptable" or so-so people, but no one that I was totally excited about until my trip to the United States of America after my National Youth Service Corps year. That was when I met Tunde.

During my final year at the University of Lagos, Nigeria, I obtained a summer internship at the National

Oil Company. While working there, I became good friends with one of the secretaries, Mary, in the department where I was assigned to work. We started going out to lunch together and got to know each other. I found out that she was planning and saving up for her first trip abroad in the summer to go to New York to visit her first cousin. I thought that was an interesting coincidence because I was also planning to take my summer trip abroad later in the summer to go to London, see my brother Omo, and then go on to Houston, TX, to visit my friend Funke, who had just moved there. I was then going from Houston to Washington, D.C., to visit my other friend, my best friend from high school, Mfon.

During our discussion, Mary convinced me it would be great if I could stop in New York on my flight from London and spend a few days with her at her cousin's place in New York before going to Houston to see my friend. I agreed and re-arranged my ticket accordingly. I only had brief stops or day visits to New York previously and was excited to spend a few days there with my friend Mary. We flew out of Lagos on the same day. Mary flew directly to New York, and I flew to London first to spend a couple of weeks there visiting my brother and his family.

After those weeks were up, I then flew to New York City, where Mary and her cousin very kindly met and received me at the airport, and we drove back to the cousin's apartment in New York City. I found out that the cousin's elderly mother was also visiting from Nigeria on her very first trip abroad, which was also her first plane

54

ride! Mary's cousin and his brother, who also lived in New York City, had planned a celebration party to mark their mother's visit to New York City and had invited all their friends to meet and celebrate their mother.

The party was on the Saturday after I arrived. Since I was also a guest at the cousin's apartment, I was not only invited to attend but immediately recruited into the party planning committee! Mary and I helped with food preparation and decorating the venue. Since the party hosts were young men mainly inviting their friends, the party for their elderly mother turned out to be a disco party with one of their friends as the DJ playing all the latest hit songs. While their mother was the guest of honor and got to meet all their friends who attended the party and even received gifts from some of the guests, the theme of the party and the music was undoubtedly for the enjoyment of the younger people.

The guests consisted of a lot of the cousins' Nigerian friends in New York City, friends from their universities, neighbors, and some relatives who had come in from out of town to see their mother. After all the guests had eaten and speeches had been made by the cousins and other relatives welcoming their mother to New York City and thanking everyone for coming to the celebration, the older cousin then opened the floor by dancing with his mother.

After the celebrant had danced with both her sons and some other relatives present, the DJ announced that the floor was officially open for the disco party for the younger guests. I had been introduced to several friends of Mary's cousins since I arrived in New York City and met a lot more at the party. Several of their friends asked me to dance over the course of the night, and I had a good time meeting many people and enjoying the time with my friend Mary.

For further context, this incident occurred in the early 1980s, specifically in the summer of 1981. At that time, people did not just go on the dance floor unless they had a partner, so men would ask the ladies to dance with them, and if, for any reason, the lady declined, the man would usually return to his seat or find another partner.

I danced with several new acquaintances, but then a young man I had not previously met came up and asked me to dance. I politely accepted, and while we were dancing, he introduced himself and said he attended New York University with the younger cousin. He then said that he could almost swear that my ancestors were from Nigeria and could help me trace my roots without doing any DNA tests! I was immediately amused and quite intrigued by this young man and his strange, bold statements. So, I decided to play along because he had obviously assumed that I was African American.

CHAPTER TWELVE

Tracing My Roots

S o, I smiled and asked how he could be so sure where my ancestors had come from or be able to help me trace my roots, or was that the standard pickup line he used with all the ladies? He laughed and assured me that it was not a pickup line at all. Apparently, I bore an uncanny resemblance to a young man who had attended the same university as him back in Nigeria. He said the resemblance was so strong that he would have sworn that the young man and I were related if I had not been African American. Nevertheless, he felt sure that my roots would most likely be connected to the tribe and lineage of this young man to whom he claimed I bore such a great resemblance.

By that point, I was completely intrigued and curious to learn more, particularly because three of my older brothers had attended two of the largest universities in Nigeria. As we continued dancing, I asked him to tell me more about his university in Nigeria and the young man who could possibly be part of my ancestral lineage.

He happily obliged, telling me that before coming to the United States of America, he had obtained his bachelor's degree from the University of Ife in Nigeria and that one of the students who ran for student council one year was the young man to whom he felt I bore such a strong resemblance. I asked him if he remembered the young man's name, to which he responded, "Of course I remember. His name is Wole Olufon".

I stopped dancing and started laughing in shock and amazement. Up to that point, we had not been formally introduced, and we had yet to introduce ourselves. My dance partner looked at me, puzzled, as I stood on the dance floor laughing. He asked me what he said that was so funny. I responded by telling him that he had not introduced himself or told me his name but instead had made the outrageous claim of helping me trace my roots. He immediately apologized for his omission and explained that he had come over to ask me to dance because he had been so struck and intrigued by my resemblance to the young man at his old university and felt he had to come over and tell me.

He then introduced himself as Tunde, a friend of Mary's younger cousin. I shook his hand and said I was pleased to meet him. I turned and started walking off the dance floor back to my seat. Still puzzled, he followed me back to my seat and asked if he had offended me. I smiled and said no, asking why he would think he had offended me. He answered that I had not told him why I was laughing and did not reciprocate by introducing myself to him. I paused for several minutes, visibly heightening the tension as the puzzled look on his face deepened.

After a long and dramatic pause, I said very slowly that he had not offended me in any way and that I was indebted to him because he had accomplished exactly what he told me he would: to help me trace my roots. Then I paused again, at which time he jumped in and started apologizing profusely, saying that if his statement or comment had been inappropriate in any manner, he was sorry and that maybe he should not presume that every African American was searching for their roots, maybe he should not have said that before getting to know me better.

I raised my hand to stem his apology speech and told him that he had led me straight to my African roots and I would be forever grateful to him. He looked even more puzzled and confused as I reached out my hand to introduce myself. "My name is Jola Olufon of the Olufon Roots Tribe."

His shout of "What?" could be heard all over the room, and the look on his face was priceless! Afterward, he ascertained that I was not putting him on and that I was really Wole's sister, the young man at his university that he spoke about, and that I was not African American. He did not dance again the rest of the night but sat down and talked with me the rest of the night, marveling at the chances that what just happened between us happened.

CHAPTER THIRTEEN

Long-Distance Courtship

The rest of the night flew by as we talked and got to know one another, both of us marveling over the unusual way we met. When it was time for him to leave the party, he asked if he could come and take me out and show me New York City the next day. I thanked him but informed him I was leaving the next day to fly to Texas. He tried to convince me to change my flight and delay my departure for a day or two, but I declined and insisted that I needed to depart for Houston as planned, as my friend had already made plans for my arrival.

He then asked if I would be willing to stop in New York City on my way back from Houston before flying back home to Lagos, Nigeria. Again, I declined, explaining to him that I was flying from Houston to Washington, DC, to visit with another friend and would then fly back home to Lagos, Nigeria, from Washington, DC. Once he realized I could not be persuaded to change my plans, he asked if we could exchange information and stay in touch.

Since this was 1982, long before everyone had their own cell phones, I gave him the telephone number of my friend Funke's house in Houston, TX, where I would be staying. Shortly after I arrived at my friend's house in Houston, TX, from the airport, Tunde called me the next day. My friend was immediately intrigued and curious to know all about this young man I had just met, who was already calling me as soon as I arrived in town. She wanted to know who this "eager beaver" was and if I had agreed to "date" him. I laughed and assured her that we were simply friends as I had just met him the day before at the celebration party in New York City.

Since she was curious, I told her the funny story of his bold declaration upon meeting me, thinking that I was African American and that he could help me trace my roots. After listening to the story and his attempts to convince me to come back to New York City, she immediately declared that this guy seemed to want more than friendship. I laughed again and reminded her that I didn't do long-distance relationships and that he was just a nice guy I had met in an unusual and interesting manner and was willing to be friends with. She was unconvinced and gave me that smug, "I told you so" look every time the phone rang, and it was Tunde calling. The phone calls happened every day while I was there, and sometimes, he called twice a day!

Tunde called me frequently after I left Houston for Washington, DC, and finally asked me before I left DC if we could officially start a dating relationship. I laughed and told him again that I did not believe in long-distance relationships for all the obvious reasons and that while I thought he was a very nice guy, I believed it best that we should remain friends and pursue relationships where we were physically located.

Interestingly, he disagreed, stating he was convinced that I was "the one for him" and that he would complete his master's program in less than two years, and he planned to move back to Lagos, Nigeria, to seek employment and live there. He suggested that we date long distance while he finished his master's program and get to know each other by exchanging letters regularly. I again stated my aversion to long-distance relationships, particularly with someone I met one time at a party and did not know anything about. I teased him that for all I knew, he may already have a wife and kids in New York, a fiancé, or a serious girlfriend, and I would have no way of knowing.

Also, I was a bit skeptical at his declaration of love and knowing I was "the one for him" after one admittedly unusual meeting, but nonetheless, one face-to-face meeting followed by several telephone conversations. While I thought he was an attractive young man with a very engaging and humorous personality, I certainly did not feel like he was "the one," nor was I ready to commit to a dating relationship with a stranger I knew nothing about.

Tunde acknowledged my concerns and asked me if I would commit to corresponding and getting to know each other for at least one year and then decide. I thought that sounded reasonable, so I agreed to correspond, keep an open mind, and give the relationship a chance.

That started our long-distance relationship between New York City and Lagos, Nigeria. I began receiving cards and letters regularly from New York City, and considering that this was the early 1980s, a regular letter from the United States took two to three weeks to arrive in Lagos, Nigeria; he made sure that he sent me a card or a letter at least two to three times a month.

It took only a few months of a steady stream of romantic cards and letters pledging unwavering love and devotion to win me over, cause me to abandon my aversion for long-distance relationships, and fully commit to this particular long-distance relationship.

To allay my fears of not knowing anything about him, Tunde arranged for his sister to contact me and introduce herself to me. She then invited me to visit their home and meet their mother, father, and their other siblings. I accepted her invitation, and when I visited her, she introduced me to their mother, who greeted me with a big smile and stated, "So, you are the young lady that my son has been raving about!" I nervously laughed as I curtsied to greet her in accordance with our culture. It was a pleasant visit, and I met some of the other siblings before I left. His sister and I became good friends and stayed in touch.

That was not the end of the introductions, however. Tunde had two of his close friends, who had attended the same university as him, contact and introduce themselves to me. With this barrage of affirmation, attention, and unrelenting pursuit, I was ultimately won over and excitedly looking forward to my prince charming's visit home for the holidays.

Tunde came home for Christmas that year, and while he was in town, he officially introduced me to his family and several of his close friends with whom he had attended university. We visited several of his friends together, and one friend who had been his roommate at the university commented that he had not seen his friend so much in love and committed to a relationship since he had known him. The other friend, Kehinde, was an attorney and worked in a law firm in Lagos, so we stopped by his firm to see him and say hello.

While we were there, he asked me which law firm I would work for now that I had passed the bar exam and had been called to the bar. I had also completed my National Youth Service Corp responsibility and was now free to work as an attorney. I responded that I was not yet working at a firm but planned to join my brother Wole, who had graduated from the University of Ife several years before, also from the faculty of Law, and had started his own law firm.

Tunde's friend Kehinde then informed me that his firm had an opening they were trying to fill at that time, and he invited me to meet the senior partner and founder of the law firm to interview for the position. We agreed on a time and set an appointment for me to come back and meet his senior partner. I did and was offered the position after the interview on the spot, and I was informed that I could start as soon as I wanted to. Since my brother was not quite ready to hire an associate at that time, nor was he in a position to pay me a salary, I decided to accept the position and work in that law firm till he was ready to hire me.

I started work at the law firm the following week, the law firm of Onagoruwa & Co., in Ebute Metta, Lagos, Nigeria. I accepted the job thinking that I would work there for a while, gain some experience, and then go back to join forces with my brother Wole, who would then be ready and able to bring on another attorney and have enough business to pay me a salary. I developed a great mentoring relationship with the founding attorney, my employer, Dr. Olu Onagoruwa, and ended up staying and working at the firm for the next six years.

CHAPTER FOURTEEN

The Vow

That Christmas before Tunde returned to New York City, we had been corresponding regularly for six months, and he had formally introduced me to his family and friends; we were now officially in a committed dating relationship and very much in love with each other. When he started talking about future plans and the timeline for getting engaged, I told him that I needed to share something with him that was very important and that he needed to know before we moved further into the relationship.

Before I met Tunde, I had dated another guy while I was at the University of Lagos and up till the commencement of my National Youth Service Corps. I started dating Remi, even though I was not attracted to him because he pursued me and was nice. I did not realize then that the sadness, sorrow, and loneliness that I felt continuously stemmed from the spirit of mourning that had come upon me after my father's sudden homegoing. The man that I loved above any other had suddenly departed, and

I was at a point in my life where none of the guys I liked or felt attracted to seemed interested in me. So, I agreed to go out with Remi, thinking that I would at least have an escort and not feel unwanted and alone, so I compromised and went into a relationship with someone I knew was not "the one" for me.

After the relationship ended, I resolved not to shortchange myself or compromise ever again. Shortly after this, my mother told me she needed to discuss an important matter with me. She informed me that a certain seer had informed her that he had a vision concerning my future. He had foreseen that unless "certain spiritual measures or steps" were immediately taken on my behalf, I would have an unplanned pregnancy, be unmarried, and end up having the child out of wedlock. That was not the news I expected to hear!

I felt like someone was trying to speak a curse upon me, and when my mother suggested we meet with the seer to find out what the recommended remedial spiritual measures were, I resisted, stating that I did not want to meet with the seer. I asked her to tell him to pray against it since the vision came from him and told her we should also pray against it ourselves as good Christians. Not to mention, I also had an aversion for seers from what we called "white garment churches," who were notorious for manipulating and exploiting people with their visions and prophecies of doom.

So, I told my mother that we should pray about his evil vision, and I would take it as a warning to be careful and to remain celibate until marriage. Sounds like a simple solution to the evil vision, right? If I do not become intimate with anyone, then I could not get pregnant and have a child out of wedlock, right?

But what about situations where you have been dating for a while, that could be six months, one year, or two years, and you are now considered "a couple," and all expectations from you and everyone else is that you will be getting married soon? How do you handle that waiting period when you are perceived as a couple, act as a couple, and do everything as a couple, but you are not officially and legally married? Is it okay then to go a little further while hugging, kissing, or petting? After all, you are now spending virtually all your spare time with each other during this courtship period and lots of time alone.

I have seen what could happen in almost all those situations with my friends and classmates. In nearly every case, couples went further than they originally intended because if you keep applying heat to water, it will boil! So, to avoid this scenario in the future, I came up with the brilliant idea that I would make a vow to God! Yes, I thought that would solve this problem perfectly!

I would make a vow to God that I would not be physically intimate with anyone until our wedding night. I thought at the time that this was the perfect solution to make sure that the white-garment seer's vision concerning me would never come to pass, and it would also give me resolve in any compromising situation. After making the vow, I decided that before becoming involved in any other serious relationship in the future, I would tell the person about my vow and ask if they were willing to respect and abide by it. If they were not willing to respect my vow to wait, then I would not become involved with them. If they agreed and supported my vow to wait till we were married, then I would know without a shadow of a doubt they were the real deal, the Real McCoy, my knight in shining armor, and that would seal the deal to move forward. Brilliant strategy, right?

CHAPTER FIFTEEN

The Vow Conversation

I was about to enter into a committed relationship with this young man I had met in New York, who had persistently pursued me from the day we met. I had received a card or note from him at least once a month when I returned to Nigeria. This feat was remarkable because it was in 1982 when mail from the US to Lagos could take anywhere from two weeks to two months to arrive. This was the true era of 'snail mail,' when much of the mail was shipped, and correspondence was not instant.

Tunde had convinced me that he wanted us to be together in a committed relationship going forward. He was about to complete his master's program and was planning to move back home to Lagos, Nigeria, the following year, 1983. So, I planned to tell him about my vow when he returned and get his agreement and assurance that there would be no intimacy between us till our wedding night. I was nervous and excited at the same time; I had grown to like this young man and felt that we could have a very good future together. Based on what I knew about him from our correspondence and our long-distance relationship, he was a gentleman and a very sincere and pleasant young man. He had expressed numerous times how much he cared about me and wanted to spend the rest of his life with me, so I was very hopeful that he would agree to respect my vow and abide by the terms of it, that there would be no intimacy between us till our wedding night.

After he moved back home to Lagos and all the initial excitement and celebration of his return had worn down, we had some alone time to talk. I informed him that there was something very important that I needed to share with him before we moved forward, and we agreed to meet the next day when we could speak without interruption and in private. He asked me if I was trying to break up with him, and I reassured him that was not the reason for the meeting or my intention. He said I was making him nervous, but he would take my word that it was not a break-up meeting and wait to hear what I wanted to share with him the next day.

Tunde decided to drive out to a scenic spot where we could talk privately and without interruption. It was a beautiful sunny day, and the overhang was at the crest of the road overlooking the lagoon. No other cars or people were around. There was just a gentle breeze blowing off the lagoon and birds singing in the trees nearby. It seemed such a perfect idyllic day to deal with a thorny issue. After a long silence, I started by telling him what a great person I thought he was and that I felt our relationship had great potential for the future. However, I had to share important information with him before we went any further. I then told him about the white-garment seer and his vision to my mother that I would become pregnant and have a child out of wedlock. Even though I did not trust or believe the white-garment seer and had refused to meet with him or participate in his suggested "spiritual preventive measures," I had assured my mother that I would take the vision/prediction as a warning and conduct myself appropriately.

Therefore, I had made a vow to God that I would not be intimate with anyone until my wedding day. So, if anyone I was dating was not willing or agreeable to abide by my vow, we could not continue the relationship. I thought telling him about my vow was only fair before we got deeper into the dating relationship. He was silent for a long while after I stopped talking, just looking at the view in the distance.

Once Tunde gathered his thoughts, he asked me questions:

When did I make the vow? Was it before we met?

I answered, "Yes."

Had I dated other guys since I made the vow?

I told him, "No."

Had I dated other guys before the vow?

Answer "yes."

Was I still a virgin, or had I been intimate before the vow?

What!? Even though I had half-expected that he would ask me that question, I was still flustered, put out, upset, and somewhat conflicted about answering this question.

You see, I was a firm believer in women's rights and equality and firmly believed and professed that a woman did not have to divulge any details of her past relationships to any man. I felt that her past before she met him was not his business, in the sense that he did not have a right to demand she share all the details of her past with him as a precondition for commitment. However, under the present unusual circumstances, I reluctantly agreed that the question was reasonable, and the answer was, "No, I am not a virgin."

Before he could question me further, I added that even though I had slipped up in the past and gone too far, that did not change the present facts. I had made a vow to God that going forward, I would no longer be intimate with anyone until my wedding night, and I fully intended to keep my vow to God. I acknowledged that my decision put him on the spot and would affect our relationship in a major way, and that was why I wanted him to know now so he could decide if he wanted to continue with the relationship. We sat in silence for a very long time, and finally, he started the car and drove me back home.

Neither of us uttered a word throughout the drive, and when we got to my parents' house where I lived, he did not turn off the engine or come in as he had done in the past. He merely turned towards me, looked me straight in the eye, and said he would need some time to think about it and make a decision. He said goodbye and drove off, leaving me pondering our outcome.

Even though I had told myself to prepare for any eventuality, I felt something unpleasant come over me. I knew the reality was that most guys would not agree to a non-sexual intimacy relationship and may choose to find someone with less stringent conditions and rules. I told myself this would help me eliminate and sort out the frogs faster until I found my prince! The part I was not fully prepared for was how sad and disappointed I felt as I watched him drive away.

Somewhere in my imagination, when I had played out the scene when I told him about my vow, I had imagined a different ending. I had imagined him saying that even though it would be difficult, he loved me so much that he would do whatever he had to do for us to be together for all time. In my romanticized imagination, he had agreed to help me keep my vow, and we would make it through our courtship period to our glorious wedding night.

CHAPTER SIXTEEN

The Reality

The reality was that Tunde drove away, saying he needed time to think. He drove off with that unspoken "don't call me, I'll call you" attitude. I watched my brand new, exciting romance crumble before my eyes, and I was taken aback by the intense feelings of sadness, rejection, disappointment, and loneliness that overwhelmed me. I had to deal with the voices in my head telling me I would never find anyone who would ever agree to abide by my crazy vow. *Why should they?* It wasn't like I was a virgin preserving my virtue till my wedding night, and why would they stay if there were lots of other girls better looking than me willing not to impose any restrictions?

I began to doubt myself and wish I had never made the vow. Then I thought, the reality is that I did make a vow, so I had no choice now but to keep it, even if it cost me this relationship. I decided that if this relationship ended abruptly because of my vow, then in my future relationship, I would make sure not to get emotionally involved before revealing my vow. I decided that was the answer. Before feelings could grow too deep, I would discuss the vow before moving forward!

I tried to comfort myself with the thought of my plan as I did not see or hear from Tunde for almost two weeks, which was a dramatic change from seeing him nearly every day before our 'vow' conversation. I told family members and friends who asked me about him that we had broken up, and I did my best to put on a "life goes on" face and told them I was okay.

I told myself that if that was all it took for him to turn tail and run, he was definitely not the person I wanted to spend the rest of my life with because his values and priorities were messed up. It helped me feel better, put on a stiff upper lip, and hold up my head as I went about my days and moved on with my life.

Then, one evening, unexpectedly, Tunde drove up and walked into the house, announcing that we needed to talk. I sat there and calmly said, "Okay," without letting my excitement or pleasure at seeing him again show in my voice or on my face. Moreover, I didn't know whether the talk would be positive or negative. I listened as he started by saying that he had been thinking a lot about our last conversation about my vow and had some questions.

We talked for the next couple of hours, discussing his questions, which ranged from what we could or could not do to how far we could go while we courted. The synopsis of our discussion was that he wanted us to be in a committed relationship. However, he was afraid. He did not know at the beginning how long our courtship may be, given that he just completed his master's program and had returned to Lagos to live at home with his parents while he searched for a job as they supported him financially. Furthermore, after finding a job, he would have to save up enough money to buy himself a car and then get a place of his own so he could move out of his parents' home and support a wife.

Given the circumstances, I thought his questions and concerns were reasonable and understandable. I obviously could not answer all his questions because I had not considered the different scenarios or issues he had raised. Tunde concluded the discussion by declaring that he wished I had not made the vow. He didn't have all the answers as to how we would be able to keep it as the courtship progressed. Still, he understood that it was important to me to honor my vow, and since he was in love with me and wanted our relationship to continue, he would agree to help me keep my vow.

When he made that declaration, I gleefully thought he had passed the test and was the one! It was even better than I had imagined in my fantasy because he was very honest with me about how much he struggled with continuing the relationship under the conditions of the vow; that he had never been in a celibate relationship before and was concerned about agreeing to wait, not knowing how long the wait would be. To me, his honesty and openness over his fears, concerns, and trepidation about committing to the relationship under the conditions of my vow only made me trust and appreciate that he had chosen me and our relationship and chose not to find someone else with no restrictions.

I naively thought that we had crossed the hardest bridge by him agreeing to keep my vow and that all the other details would be sorted out as we progressed. I thought that since we had both committed to each other, loved and trusted each other, the rest of the details would fall into place. Oh, how wrong I was!

CHAPTER SEVENTEEN

The Best Laid Plans

In the first few weeks after the discussion and mutual decision to move forward into a committed relationship, agreeing to keep the vow, we were excited and happy to be back together with a stronger love and appreciation for each other. We even felt that the vow would strengthen us because we were working on it together, and there were no secrets or barriers between us. We giggled and laughed at whether we should kiss, when to kiss, how long we could kiss, how long we could hug, how late we could be out together, and what places to go. We treated it like an adventure in setting boundaries, and it was fun and exciting.

This idyllic fairy tale period lasted about three months, and then things began to change. The boundaries became too restrictive, and the pressure was rising, as Tunde thought that the boundaries we had set should become less restrictive. A trip out of town to be introduced to his father did not help, as we stayed the night at his father's house, and they put us both in one room with a tiny bed and no couch. That night changed everything because even though we survived the night without breaking the vow, neither of us got much sleep as we argued over how far we could go without going too far.

When we returned to Lagos, Tunde decided we should get engaged, which would be enough to remove the barriers. I disagreed and said that my vow was non-sexual intimacy till my wedding night. He then suggested that we go ahead and get married secretly at the marriage registry by ourselves without telling our families so that we could get rid of the vow but still give our families time to plan the big traditional church wedding that was customary and expected. The suggestion was tempting as the tension between us was rising higher and higher, and the focus every time we met had become how to get rid of or satisfy the vow.

However, I did not want a secret marriage, just to be intimate. I had dreams of how my wedding day would be and the beautiful honeymoon afterward, and I was not prepared to trade that dream for a quick secret wedding now, a back-alley wedding night, and then a pretend big wedding afterward. So, I compromised. No secret marriage, but since we were now engaged and preparing to be married, we could relax the boundaries just a little more; we could go further, but not all the way.

Big mistake! Once you get on the slippery slope, it's downhill from there! You think you are in control, but the further you agree to go, the further he still wants to go, and then he claims that he can't stop and pushes past all agreed barriers. Once you cross the barrier the first time, there's no longer any barrier or reason for celibacy, just excuses, apologies, regrets, and consequences.

The consequences, in this instance, were quick. I discovered, barely a couple of months after we broke the vow, that I was pregnant. Tunde said, "No problem." The plan then was to move the wedding date forward so we could get married before the baby arrived. Surely our families would cooperate and speed up the plans and arrangements so we could hold the ceremony before I started to show or at least before the baby arrived?

I didn't know it then, but a satanic drama of epic proportions was about to unfold, a drama that engulfed me like a dark cloud and would almost destroy me.

CHAPTER EIGHTEEN

Life's Banquet Table of Consequences

E ven though I was dealing with the guilt that I had broken my vow and, as a consequence, I was pregnant, I consoled myself. I had asked God to forgive me, and we were proceeding to get married speedily. God was understanding and forgiving, and everything was going to be alright.

We agreed that we would talk to his mother and let her know that we were expecting and would like to expedite the traditional marriage process, which in our culture precedes the church wedding ceremony, and that we would like to get married within three to four months.

Tunde seemed confident that there would not be any problems as he had just been hired by the Nigerian National Petroleum Company (NNPC) as a chemical engineer, and he was confident that he would find an apartment and move out of his parent's home before the wedding. Also, with his new job, he had medical insurance that would cover me and the baby. It looked like everything would work out just fine, and I would have a great wedding like I had always wanted, albeit a bit faster and quicker than we had anticipated. Nevertheless, we would be married and starting a family immediately afterward.

I chose to go along with his optimistic view that there would be no problems and that his mother would be happy and excited about the baby and glad to help speed up the arrangements. I suppressed the gnawing fear in the pit of my stomach, that taunting, tormenting voice that kept telling me that there was not going to be a wedding and that his mother was not going to be happy or excited about the baby or any wedding plans and would certainly not help speed up any arrangements. The taunting voices kept telling me I had fallen into the trap set for me and fulfilled the evil prophecy the white-garment seer gave. Even while I was shouting down and suppressing the tormenting voices in my head, I could not stop the replay in my mind of some recent incidences that had troubled me, and those incidents involved his mother.

In the beginning, I felt very welcome. Everyone from Tunde's mother to his stepfather and all his siblings received me with enthusiasm and kindness, and I loved to visit their home and hang out with them. However, I started noticing changes in warmth and friendliness, particularly from his mother, while we struggled with the vow. But I thought it had to be my imagination since he had assured me he did not discuss our struggles concerning the vow with anyone. It was quickly confirmed to me that it was not just my imagination during a visit to his family's home, a short while later when his mother not only pointedly ignored me after sarcastically referring to me as "Miss Lawyer," a departure from the old greeting of "my daughter," that she had used in the past. Not only that, she then went out of her way to fuss with great exaggeration over her oldest daughter's new boyfriend, who was also visiting. It was clear her feelings about me had shifted, and the gnawing pit only grew.

After that incident, Tunde no longer dismissed my concerns but said that she was really upset with him as she felt hurt that he had given me an engagement ring without clearing it with her first! So, due to the frigid receptions, we made fewer visits to his mother's house, hence my concern and nervousness when he was going to ask her to speed up the wedding plans. But he assured me that the news of the baby would soften her, assuage her anger at him, and re-ignite the old warm relationship. I hoped he was right as I wanted a close relationship with my future mother-in-law, the kind of relationship we had when I first met her. Also, because of their unique family dynamics and history, I knew it would not work long-term, and it would be hell on earth if she chose to treat me as an adversary.

This was because Tunde had been raised by his mother as a single parent after she left his father when he was very young. His biological father had no input in his upbringing and, in fact, had not seen him from infancy till he was a young man. Tunde's father had several wives, as did many Nigerian men in those days. So, when Tunde's mother had Tunde, she felt threatened by the senior wives and thought that her and her son's lives were in danger, so she took him and ran away and never made contact with Tunde's father after that. She subsequently got married to his stepfather and had other children.

Expectedly, Tunde was very close to his mother and siblings and very grateful to his mother and stepfather for all the opportunities they provided him to further his education, including paying his way to obtain a master's degree in chemical engineering in the USA. As one would imagine, his mother was the dominant force in his life and apparently expected not only to have a say but actually control the details of his marital future. If she did not like something, I knew things would be tricky. But I did my best to take comfort in Tunde's belief that everything would be okay.

However, when Tunde returned from his meeting with his mother, his optimism was visibly shaken, even as he tried to present the facts lightly. The summation of their meeting was that she had said, "Not so fast!" The fact that I was pregnant was no reason to rush into anything, and she did not think it was proper to have a rushed wedding in three to four months just because I was pregnant.

The traditional process would start with her informing all members of their family of his intention to marry, then finding a date acceptable for their family to meet to discuss the plans to meet my family for a meet and greet. After that, both families would set mutually acceptable dates for the exchange of the formal letter of proposal of marriage signed by the head of his family and the letter of acceptance of the proposal and intent signed by the head of my family. Then, the families would set a date for the traditional engagement ceremony, also known as the traditional marriage.

This is the ceremony where the groom and his entire family, and all their friends and neighbors, come to the bride's family's home, bearing a large assortment of gifts for the bride and her family and formally ask them for their permission and blessing to take their daughter as wife for their son and make her a member of the groom's family.

This is a covenant ceremony between the families, where they pledge to care for and support the new couple and cover them in prayers. The ceremony concludes with lots of eating, drinking, and dancing after all the gifts have been exchanged and pledges made. Thereafter, the formal church wedding ceremony and reception culminates the process.

Tunde's mother suggested to him that rather than rush the process, he should wait until after I had the baby, and then they would start the process.

CHAPTER NINETEEN

A Formidable Foe

After Tunde told me his mother's suggestion, I burst into tears as the voices in my head cackled gleefully, "You're trapped, you're trapped! We told you so! She got you. There's not going to be any wedding!" My heart sank within me as I realized I was in a terrible situation and in over my head.

When Tunde saw my distress, he quickly reassured me that he disagreed with his mother's suggestion and had told her so. He had maintained that we wanted to get married before the baby arrived and still believed he could persuade her, but if she still refused, then we may have to scale back the ceremony and have a smaller wedding. He suggested we give her a little time before he spoke to her again. I could see that even his optimism was slipping, even though he still maintained that she would change her mind.

After he left that evening, I sat in a daze, stunned and incredulous that she could have made such a suggestion. However, the more I thought about it, the more I began to see how her position aligned exactly with who she was. Not only had she raised Tunde by herself before she married his stepfather, but she had also raised his older sister.

When her oldest daughter was dating a certain young man and had gotten pregnant and was planning to marry the young man, the story was that the wedding was canceled because they had received word from a seer that the young man was not her husband, and that tragic things would happen if she married him. So, the wedding was canceled, and the relationship was terminated. She stayed home with her parents, had her child, and raised him in their home.

My heart sank as I realized that what she proposed to her son was not strange for her, and since she didn't seem to like me much anymore, this was her *modus operandi*. If it happened to her daughter, why could it not happen to "Miss Lawyer"? However, I still hoped against hope that her son could persuade her to change her mind if he stood his ground and appealed to her.

I felt like a powerless pawn in a game when, several weeks later, she refused to budge and insisted that nothing be done until after the baby was born. We talked for several hours, discussing several options, and finally agreed that he would ask his father to write the letter of proposal and intent to marry as the head of his family. We would then get married in a civil ceremony before our baby was born. Tunde stated that he did not want our baby born out of wedlock, so we should forgo the big wedding ceremony and do what we needed to do for ourselves and our baby. While I was very sad at the turn of events and the fact that I was not going to have the wedding I had dreamed and hoped for, I acknowledged that I had gotten myself into this mess when I broke my vow, and the best thing to do was to move forward and do what we needed to do. At that point, I had no communication with any member of his family, and it was now obvious not only that his mother was not going to change her mind but that she had something against me, more than the fact that he gave me an engagement ring without asking her permission first.

When I pressed, Tunde stated that she was also upset that he had taken me to visit and meet his father without her permission. She blamed me for all the actions that he had taken without getting her permission and felt that he would not have taken those actions if I had not been such a bad influence on him. She said that I was arrogant and thought I was all that, hence the change in salutation from "my daughter" to "Miss Lawyer."

He opined that she would get over it, and all would be forgotten and forgiven once the baby was born. So, he intensified his search for an apartment so that he could move out of his parents' home and we could have our own accommodations. He had also decided to stop trying to persuade his mother to change her mind and just dropped the subject altogether. She apparently took this as agreement with her plan to not take any steps until after the baby was born. Eventually, he found an apartment he liked and had enough money to pay the down payment, and he started the process of moving out of his parents' house. Things calmed down once Tunde stopped trying to persuade her to change her mind, and I stopped going to their home. He waited till he had completed the move into his new apartment before telling her that he had asked his father to write the letter of intention to marry and the proposal and that we would have a civil ceremony to be married before the baby arrived.

Tunde's mother was furious and told him it was disrespectful to bypass her and his stepfather after all they had done for him, and she could not believe that he would dishonor her by going against her stated wishes. He told her he meant no disrespect or dishonor to her or his stepfather, and that was why we were not having any big ceremony, but that he did not want our child to be born out of wedlock. After an extensive argument with neither side relenting, he bid her goodnight and left for his new apartment, thinking that at least he could stay away for a while and give her time to cool off, and everything would blow over again.

Tunde could not have been more wrong. He had no concept or idea of how far his mother was willing to go to get her way. He had no idea how much she was willing to escalate the situation or what depths she would sink to maintain her control over him and make him do her bidding. What happened next can best be described as letting loose the hounds of hell.

In the days following the heated discussion with his mother, Tunde was tense and agitated several times. He complained about being unable to sleep at night and just tossing and turning all night and assumed naturally that this was due to the tension and impasse with his mother. He hoped that she would either relent before the baby was born and commence the necessary steps for the traditional marriage or, at the worst, relent after the baby was born and take the steps then. Either way, we had agreed to move forward with the letter of intent and the civil ceremony. He had also decided it would be best for him not to stop by or visit his parents' home for a while so as not to aggravate the situation.

At this point, I was close to the end of my second trimester, being about six months pregnant and, of course, very visibly showing. Even though our wedding plans were crumbling around us and the tension and uncertainty were at epic proportions, we both agreed that we would go through the civil ceremony, put everything else on hold, and focus solely on getting married and having our baby. I tried very hard to suppress all my fears and disappointment, hurt, anger and confusion, embarrassment, and yes, shame. I continuously reminded myself that I was now responsible for another human life, and I absolutely had to stay mentally and physically healthy for both our sakes.

Moreover, Tunde was already so tense, wound up, and agitated from sleeplessness that I knew that if I did not keep myself together and keep a stiff upper lip, he would snap, and everything would come apart. It was evident to me that he had never stood up to his mother or opposed her wishes for any important decision in his life. This was very difficult and was beginning to take its toll on him. But I was proud of him and thankful that he stood up as a man for his future family and insisted on doing things right.

One evening, when Tunde came by my parents' house, we discussed how the move into his new apartment was coming and his now much longer commute to work, as he now lived on the mainland while his work and his parents' home were both on the island. We also discussed his plans to go to the marriage registry during his lunch break the next day to apply for the marriage license, and once he obtained that, after the statutory wait period, we could then get married.

As Tunde was leaving to return to his apartment that night, he said with a wry smile that he was glad he took his bed and a few chairs on the first truckload of his move; otherwise, he would have had to sleep on the floor, since he had not been able to go back to his parents' house to get the rest of his things. He thanked me for the food I had packed for him to take home, as he had no pots or pans. We laughed when he said he had the two most essential things: a bed to sleep on and food to eat.

The tension and the dark clouds that had continuously overshadowed us seemed to lift for minutes as we hugged and kissed each other goodnight before he drove off.

CHAPTER TWENTY

Letting the Hellhounds Loose

L ittle did I know that was the calm before the storm. That was the last hug and kiss we would ever share; that was the last respite before the hounds of hell were unleashed upon our lives.

I arrived at the law offices where I worked the following day feeling slightly more optimistic than I had felt in a while. I sat down at my desk and was working on one of my assigned cases when Tunde came busting into my office without giving the secretary at the front office an opportunity to announce his arrival. I looked up in surprise as my office door burst open without a knock, and as soon as I saw him standing there and the look on his face, my heart sank to the pit of my stomach, and a wave of unexpected terror washed over me.

He looked disheveled and unkempt, wearing rumpled clothes and bathroom slippers, also known as flip-flops. His hair was not combed, he was unshaven, and he looked like he just got out of bed and walked out of his apartment. As if his appearance was not alarming enough, the look on his face was a thousand times worse. Even now, I still find it hard to describe the look on his face. It was bone-chilling, blood-curdling, alarming, and mournful all at the same time. I felt myself shaking with terror from the inside out, and my legs felt like they were about to give out under me. I could not understand why I was trembling with such terror, and he had not even said a word. I didn't know it then, but there was an evil presence all over him and upon him that came into my office with him and caused my reaction. He had brought an evil, very dark presence into my office that was now affecting both of us.

Tunde stood there for what seemed like an eternity and just looked at me without saying anything. I wanted to ask him what he was doing in my office at that time of morning with no prior notice and why he had not gone to work, but I could not utter a word. I felt a cold chill come over me, and my entire body was shaking. It seemed as if the tense silence lasted for hours but was probably just several minutes.

I finally broke the silence in a shaky, trembling voice, barely above a whisper, and asked him what happened. He then asked me to sit down because we needed to talk. He started by stating that he would forgive me for anything from my past if I was honest with him and told him the whole truth. I was aghast and bewildered, having no idea what he could be talking about. He stated again that there shouldn't be any secrets between us, and I could tell him what I had done in the past, and he was willing to forgive me and still move on. That was when I got mad. I jumped out of my seat and snapped at him, "Have you lost your mind? You show up at my office early in the morning looking disheveled and unkempt with a crazed look on your face, asking me to confess to, I don't know what, from my past so you can forgive me? Forgive me for what?"

My bewilderment, anger, and frustration must have been apparent as the octave of my voice got higher and higher as I demanded to know what he meant. I did not have the slightest clue what crime I had committed in my past that I was supposed to confess. He then asked me pointedly if I had consulted any seer or medicine man about our relationship or if I had specifically asked anyone to take certain steps on my behalf to ensure that he, Tunde, would marry me.

I was aghast, filled with horror and shock, dumbfounded that he would ask me such a question. I was disappointed that he would even ask me that question, knowing that in the two years since we met, he spent one year convincing me to agree to commit to a long-distance relationship and even decide if I liked him enough to commit to a serious relationship. After all, he was not what you would call a "prize catch" by any stretch of the imagination. He had not had a job, a car of his own, any independent wealth, and certainly didn't "come from money." So, why on earth would I consult anyone to take steps to ensure he married me? If the situation were not so insane, it would be comical. What baffled me the most was why he would believe his mother's obvious made-up plot, knowing all the above and that she was desperate to have her way. Why would he show up at my office early in the morning looking disheveled just to ask me questions about what he should have seen as a blatant lie?

Then Tunde dropped the other shoe, or more appropriately, he dropped the bombshell. He stated that his mother had shown up at his apartment before dawn, banging on his door. After he let her in, still half asleep, she proceeded to tell him that her reasons for advising him not to rush into marriage with me were for his own good and based on specific facts that had been brought to her attention. She then told him that a certain spiritualist with whom she was acquainted had informed her that I had approached a spiritualist and asked his assistance to ensure that my boyfriend, who was returning home from America, would marry me and that the spiritualist had given me some potions and other things to use on him.

She told Tunde that was why he was so besotted with me and would not listen to anything she had to say. He told her he did not believe her since he knew I did not believe in or consult spiritualists. He reminded her I had not fully committed to the relationship until he returned home and convinced me he was serious. She told him that was all part of the plan the spiritualist gave me, along with the potions he had made to achieve the purpose. When Tunde still insisted that he did not believe her, she asked him if she took him to the spiritualist I had allegedly consulted and if he could hear the facts directly from the spiritualist's mouth, if he would believe her then. She told him to get in the car with her right then, and she would take him there and prove the facts to him.

Tunde agreed to go with her. He got in the car with her, and her driver drove them both to a house in Ebute Metta, Lagos, located barely five minutes from the law firm where I worked! They then proceeded to a small dark room in the back of the house, and a man draped in a robe who looked like a spiritualist confirmed to him that it was true that a tall, fair-complexioned girl fitting my description had come to him for help to ensure that her boyfriend, Tunde, who would soon return home from abroad, would marry her.

The spiritualist assured him that the girl had not requested anything to harm him, just a love potion to ensure he married her, and that was not uncommon in his trade for young ladies to make such a request. Tunde then left the spiritualist's house in a daze, refused to get back into his mother's car, and walked to my office.

I could feel the blood drain from my body as I started to shiver and shake while he concluded by repeating that he was willing to forgive me for anything I had done in the past if I just told him the truth. Processing the story, I stood there shivering in fear, dumbfounded, as it dawned on me that his mother would stop at nothing to destroy me and the relationship to get her way. I could not believe the elaborate evil scheme she had concocted to keep him under her control. I was speechless and stupefied, overwhelmed by the implications of this well-concocted, evil charade his mother had orchestrated. I could not believe to what depths she would sink or lengths she would go to coerce his obedience and to maintain her control over him.

I started to cry uncontrollably as the enormity of what I was involved in dawned on me. I could feel and sense the presence of evil right there in my office, an evil, suffocating presence there with us. As I continued to cry uncontrollably, unable to respond, Tunde kept saying that I should tell him the truth and that we would put it behind us and move forward as we had planned. In other words, he already believed his mother's story. *How could he not have believed her?* He just wanted me to admit to it as it was inconceivable to him that his mother would put together such an elaborate charade.

The plot was designed to force him to choose whether to believe his mother or me, a girl he had known for less than two years. Suddenly, I knew deep in my heart that this was the beginning of the end, not just of the immediate wedding plans but the entire relationship. I cried even more uncontrollably as I realized what a dark, formidable foe I was up against and how much over my head and alone I was in this struggle. I stood there trembling and weeping, thinking it could not get any worse. Oh, but it did!

Tunde announced that he had a suggestion for resolving the whole matter. He then proposed that I go back to the Spiritualist's Den with him to confront the man and tell him to his face that I was not the person who had consulted him or requested a love potion. That perchance, once the man saw me, he would realize his mistake, and the whole matter would be resolved as a mistaken identity.

I considered his suggestion for one fleeting second, but that insanity only lasted one second. What would it resolve, and for whom? This situation was no case of mistaken identity. This was a well-orchestrated and choreographed charade put together by his mother to destroy our relationship and any credibility I had with him as well. If I were foolhardy and stupid enough to follow him into the den of evil and witchcraft, then my blood would be on my own head.

I became indignant that Tunde asked me to confront his mother's witch doctor in the witch doctor's lair. He could not possibly have my welfare or the welfare of our baby as his priority. After a few more minutes of futile argument, he left, saying he needed to get by himself to clear his head. As he walked out of my office with a dazed, confused look on his face, I burst into tears again, overwhelmed by the enormity of his mother's actions and the ramifications of it. I trembled with fear and dread as the implications of what had just transpired dawned on me.

CHAPTER TWENTY-ONE

The Lowest Point of My Life

With Tunde gone, I stood next to the window of my third-floor office at the law firm, crying and trying to make sense of and understand what had just happened in my life. My fiancée's mother had just accused me of soliciting and procuring a witch doctor's love potion to cause her son to become besotted with me and insist on marrying me despite his mother's opposition to the union. Not only did she accuse me of this heinous, despicable act, but she went further to furnish her son, my fiancé, with "evidence" to support her accusations. Thus, it was no longer just her word against mine; she had furnished corroboration.

Corroboration is evidence that confirms or supports a statement, theory, or finding; Corroboration is confirmation. As an attorney, I marveled at her evil genius and how adroit this checkmate move was. Her corroborating witness, the spiritualist, was located conveniently close to my office, which increased the probability of the veracity of their story, raising the odds that he would stick to the story they had agreed upon and for which I had no doubt he had been handsomely paid and rewarded.

I remembered that from the time of Jesus in the Bible, and since then, a second corroborating witness was required to convict a person. That was why they had to devise witnesses against Jesus to convict him. The Bible states in 2 Corinthians 13:19 (KJV), *"In the mouth of two or three witnesses shall every word be established."* Not only had she produced a strong second witness, but she had also produced the best and most convincing corroborative witness, the one who not only claimed that he heard or saw the alleged action but also claimed to have been the accused's accomplice!

How was anyone supposed to handle a situation like this? I stood there shivering and overwhelmed with fear at the realization that I was way out of my league and outnumbered. I was stunned at how far and how low she would go to ensure that her son did not marry me, even with a baby on the way. As I looked out my office window on the 3rd floor, down at the open gutter with debris and murky water on the ground floor, the futility of my situation washed all over me and almost choked me.

It seemed the devil had me just where he wanted me: surrounded and trapped, pregnant, alone, and accused, and as far as I was concerned, already convicted and abandoned. I thought of the grief and shame I would bring upon myself and my family as an unwed mother; I thought how unfair it was to any child to be born into this messy, toxic situation and out of wedlock. As the dark clouds enveloped me, my thoughts spiraled lower and lower, and I felt the cold grip of despair and hopelessness washing over me. I thought it would be better to end it and spare us all the shame, pain, and embarrassment to come. I looked down at the gutter, three floors down, and the concrete floor around it and wondered if I should end it all. After all, I had let God down. I had broken my vow and played right into the devil's hands. I had let my family and myself down, became pregnant out of wedlock, and dashed all my hopes and dreams of having a dream wedding with all my family, my siblings, friends, all our neighbors, and everyone who knew me present, rejoicing and celebrating me.

How did I get to this place? How did I go from being that bright-eyed, excited, smart, and ambitious can-doer who could conquer the world, attain any position, and do anything she set her mind to do to this dejected, shamefaced, accused and abandoned, scared, confused and desperate girl, wondering if she should end it all?

I could hear a mocking voice telling me, "You should have listened to the white-garment seer and followed his counsel instead of making your foolish and arrogant vow of celibacy. See where that has gotten you now! You're not so smart! You're nothing! Nobody wants you, and now it's all over for you!" As the mocking voice badgered and tormented me, I felt myself shrinking lower and lower, feeling overpowered by the hate and the rejection. Then I thought of my fiancé, who had just left my office, looking disheveled, unkempt, and confused, my knight in shining armor, the one I had chosen to spend the rest of my life with, the father of our unborn child who I had hoped would protect, defend and love me and our children for the rest of our lives. The husband, father, and head of our household had just walked out, looking like a man with the rug pulled from under him. He looked like a man who had been checkmated and defeated.

Reflecting on our conversation, I wryly thought that one could summarize the encounter as follows: he gave me two options. To either admit that I had done what his mother accused me of, confess my sin to him so he could forgive me, and we can move forward, or go with him back to the evil witch doctor's den, confront and contradict the witch doctor to his face and make him retract. To his way of thinking, it was my responsibility and even duty to take either of the options he gave me to resolve the situation and move us forward.

The irony of the situation hit me while I was standing at the window. There was an incongruity between what was expected and what was actually happening. I had gone from the girl who was not interested in dating this person, the girl who was being pursued and heavily courted and persuaded to commit to this relationship, to being accused of procuring the potions and powers of a witch doctor to snare and entrap him! Once more, I could not help but think the situation would have been comical if it had not been so tragic. Tunde had no material wealth, no house, no car, no inheritance coming to him, no fame or fortune, nothing that made him so desirable that a person would do anything to get him! He had just secured his first job! Marrying him would not be a step up for me by any stretch of the imagination.

I was the third lawyer, the first female lawyer, in my immediate family, and I was poised for a bright future and career. Why would I need a back-alley witch doctor to entrap a husband? If I did, wouldn't I have chosen to entrap someone with wealth and status? A millionaire who could transform me from a working-class professional into a millionaire living the lifestyle of the rich and famous? One would think that it would be evident to anyone, especially him, that I was only with him because I loved him and believed we could build a good life and family together.

I concluded that his mother and the witch doctor had done something to him to put him in that confused, dazed state, and I would give him time to clear his head and get away from whatever they had done to him. I reasoned that he would come to see this for what it was: a desperate ploy of his mother to separate us, destroy our relationship, and remain in control of his life.

I decided to give him time to sort things out and do the right thing. I also decided that no matter what the outcome of this saga was, mine and my baby's future, my baby's well-being had to be my highest priority and focus and that I would survive.

CHAPTER TWENTY-TWO

The Beginning of the End

S ince I had a lot weighing on me, I left work early
that day, went home, and broke the news to my
mother and sister. I told them about his mother's
accusation and his suggestion that I either admit the
accusation or go with him to confront the witch doctor.
My mother and sister were both horrified at his mother's
reprehensible actions, her lying accusations, and also at
his response and suggestions to me. They were both very
supportive and comforting and reassured me that my
baby and I would be fine.

My sister was incredulous that he could believe his
mother's accusations, knowing how long he pursued and
courted me to convince me to commit to the relationship.
She said if anybody needed to do anything to coerce
or influence the other party, it would obviously be him!
I was reassured and calmed by my mother and sister's
support and reassurance, and the people who knew me
best thought the accusation was ridiculous and a scenario
concocted by a desperate and controlling mother. I still

held out hope Tunde would come to realize his mother's scheming ways. Though, I would soon be left reeling once more.

The next time I saw Tunde was over a week from the day of the drama at my office. He told me he thought it best for us to put our plans on hold for now. I asked him to clarify what that meant for me. How do we put a second-trimester pregnancy on hold? He stated that he thought it best to put our wedding plans on hold for now and would support whatever decision I made concerning the pregnancy.

I felt as if someone had punched me in the stomach, and I had gotten the life knocked out of me. I sat there in a daze, trying to process what he had just told me, concluding that the Cliff note version of what he just said was that he agreed with his mother, our relationship was over, and I could either have an abortion or keep the baby. Once more, I asked him again to clarify what his decision to put all plans on hold meant concerning the baby. He calmly stated that he realized that he could not force me either to have the baby or not have the baby; that had to be my decision, but he would support me 100% no matter what decision I made. I got up, told him I needed time to think, bid him goodbye, and left.

I clearly remember that the most dominant emotion I felt that day was an overwhelming sense of rejection, rejected by the one person I had chosen, above all others, to spend my life with. He had not only rejected me but our unborn child as well. He had chosen his relationship with his mother over a relationship with me and our unborn child. To make matters worse, he had left the decision as to whether our child lived or died solely in my hands without taking a stand. In retrospect, what hurt the most was that he did not fight for us, not for me or his unborn child. He did not even advocate for his child or express what his preference would have been concerning his child. Saying that he hoped that I would have the baby even though he was not moving forward with the wedding plans would have indicated to me that he still cared, at least about our child.

A dark cloud of despair settled over me as I contemplated the long, lonely, dark road ahead of me. The taunting voices in my head were telling me that not only was I a jilted bride, but I would also be an unwed mother, a double jeopardy that would ensure that nobody would marry me, sealing my fate to live the rest of my life as a forsaken spinster and unwed mother. I thought about the shame and embarrassment I would bring to my family and cried and cried and fell even deeper into despair.

I could not stop crying. I stopped going to work, leaving the house, and getting out of bed. I barely left my room. I was not able to eat as I lost all my appetite and was quickly sinking into a deep depression. By the third day of this time of darkness, my mother and my sister became very concerned and worried about my physical and mental health, and both decided to do an intervention. Early on the morning of the fourth day, around dawn, my mother and sister Iyabo came into my room, and my mother said we needed to talk. She asked me to sit up in the bed, and she opened up with prayer, asking for the Lord's wisdom for us all and His comfort and peace for me. My mother then reassured me that I was not alone, that God was with me, and so was she and all my siblings. She told me that before meeting my father, she had also had some relationships that did not work out and had found herself in circumstances not too different from mine. My mother said that God saw her through and strengthened her to go on, take care of herself and her sons, and continue her education. She made it through and later met and married my father.

My mother reminded me of my strength and the leadership qualities I had always exhibited, even from my youth. She told me how special I was and how much I was loved. She reminded me that I was the first female attorney in our family, following in my two older brothers' footsteps, who had become lawyers before me. She reassured me that my child and I would be fine, and there was still light and joy ahead of me.

I cried throughout my mother's talk, but this time, it was not tears of despair and sorrow. I could feel the heavy, dark clouds lifting, and I began to believe that there would be light at the end of this very dark tunnel. Like my mother said, I began to believe that there was still joy, purpose, and fulfillment ahead of me. I hugged my mother and sister and thanked them for their love and support and for helping to lift me up from the pit of darkness I had fallen into. My mother encouraged me to get out of bed, take a hot bath, get dressed, and come and join them for breakfast.

That day marked the beginning of my climb back to peace and a sound mind. It was still a long and arduous climb, but I knew without a shadow of a doubt that day that no matter what the final outcome of this saga was, my child and I would be fine and that my family would love and support me through whatever lay ahead.

CHAPTER TWENTY-THREE

Moving On

After a week off, I returned to work, feeling stronger and more able to cope with my situation. I had decided to tell my employer and owner of the law firm what was going on and that there would not be a wedding. He was shocked at the news but was very supportive and encouraging. He reassured me that the young man, my fiancé, would not be stupid enough to let a gem like me slip through his fingers and that he hoped things would still work out between us, but if it did not, it would be more my fiancé's loss than mine. He said I could take as much time off as needed with full pay. I also spoke to all my older siblings, who expressed their love and support for me and reassured me that all would be well.

With my family and employer's love and support, I decided to change my previous plans. I planned to go abroad to shop for my wedding and the baby, but without a wedding to prepare for, I would still go on the trip as planned but only to shop for the baby. Also, it would be a great time to get away from all the pressure and drama and spend some time away with my brother in London and my best friend from high school who was in the United States. With my family's blessing and support and my employer's approval, I left Lagos in the summer of 1984, anticipating a refreshing and rejuvenating four-week trip to London and Nashville, TN, USA.

At that time in 1984, the airlines had put some measures in place to require visibly pregnant women to obtain their doctor's clearance before boarding an international flight. There had been some incidences of pregnant women going into labor while on an international trip abroad, and on one or two occasions, the plane had to make an emergency, unscheduled landing to get the women to a hospital. Since I was about to commence my third trimester, and my due date was the end of September, I moved my trip from early August, when the peak season was over and the flights were cheaper, to early July to avoid any risk of interrogation by the airline. Planning for the trip was a welcome relief as it took my mind off the circumstances and drama going on in my life to deciding the dates and times of my flights and length of stay in each country.

At this point, interaction and communication with Tunde had become limited to the random times he would stop by to "check up on me." Since there was no longer anything much to talk about as the situation remained the same, the visits got fewer and fewer, as did the tense, awkward silences between us.

Concerning my trip abroad, I decided that if he happened to stop by before I left, I would inform him of my plans, but if not, he would be informed by my sister when he showed up. Again, this was the time before cell phones, and we had a house phone that did not give a dial tone most of the time, so communications were face-to-face and in person. He did not stop by before I left on my trip, so he found out about it two weeks after I had left the country when he showed up.

My sister later told me that he had a surprised look on his face when she informed him. He then asked her if I was planning to stay and have the baby abroad or if I was coming back home to have the baby. She told him that as far as she knew, I planned to return home to have the baby unless, for some reason, I changed my mind. My sister relayed he was not only shocked and surprised but visibly upset that I had left the country without his knowledge and maybe even permission. That was quite laughable!

I, on the other hand, felt my spirit soar as the plane took off from the airport in Lagos, Nigeria, headed for London, England. I felt the clouds lifting, and I was excited to be off on an adventure with my soon-to-be-born child. I planned to spend two weeks in London and stay with my brother and his family, and he was meeting me at the airport to pick me up. My brother had been updated about my circumstances before I left home and was well aware that there would no longer be a wedding. He, along with my other siblings, was disappointed that my fiancé had put me in such a frustrating position by not stepping up to protect me and the baby.

When I arrived at the London airport terminal, my brother was waiting for me. He gave me a big hug and reassured me that everything would be alright. I choked back the tears as I silently thanked God for my wonderful family and their amazing support and love at this low and fragile point of my life. He drove me to their home, to a nice meal prepared by my sister-in-law and an enjoyable evening getting reacquainted with my two young nieces with their adorable British accent.

My two weeks in London flew by very quickly, filled with numerous shopping trips to baby stores, where I bought all the various items I would need when the baby arrived. On one of such trips to yet another baby supply store, my brother had driven me to this store to help transport some of the heavier items. As we loaded the item into the trunk of his car, he started to laugh uproariously. He finally paused briefly in response to my puzzled look and said between bouts of laughter that in all the years I had been coming to London to shop, this was the first time I had not shopped at or even visited any of the ladies' boutiques or women's clothing stores, that I had not stopped by any of my favorite shoe or purse stores or my usual jewelry stores, but had shopped exclusively, all the two weeks at baby stores. He laughed even harder as he welcomed me to the new life of parenthood, where everything was now all about the child. I stood there, bemused, as the truth of his words hit me; my entire focus had become all about providing everything necessary for the baby's welfare. I laughed with him as I realized that I had not bought anything for myself except some maternity essentials. I joked that it would be a while before I could fit into any cute new outfits. Nonetheless, it felt really good shopping for and preparing for the arrival of my baby.

CHAPTER TWENTY-FOUR

Off to America

I truly enjoyed my two weeks in London, shopping and hanging out with my brother, sister-in-law, and two nieces. It was the middle of summer, and the weather, by London standards, was terrific. I felt like I had left all my sad thoughts and reality behind me, and I refused to entertain any of it that tried to resurface. At the end of the two weeks, my brother drove me to the airport to catch my flight to New York and then to Nashville, TN, where I planned to spend about three weeks with my best friend from high school.

My friend Mfon was a student at the dental school at Meharry Medical College in Nashville, TN. Mfon and I attended Our Lady of Apostles Secondary School in Lagos, Nigeria, from 1969 to 1973, where we became best friends. After our ordinary level, also known as the West African School Certificate Examination, which was equivalent to an American High school diploma, Mfon left Nigeria to join her two older sisters in the United States to attend college. We wrote many letters and saw each other when she came home for Christmas. After I became a student at the University of Lagos, Nigeria, I started saving up my earnings from my summer employment towards an airline ticket to travel abroad. I would then solicit contributions from my older siblings and uncles to supplement my savings, then purchase my airline ticket to spend about six weeks of my 12-week summer break in London and America.

So, from about 1977 to 1978, I started this yearly routine of working for six weeks and then traveling abroad for six weeks during the summer vacations. I would typically stop first in London and spend about two weeks with my brother Omo, then go to the States and spend two to four weeks visiting family and friends but spend the bulk of my time visiting my friend Mfon. On prior visits, I had visited Mfon in Washington, DC, when she was attending Catholic University, and then on another trip, I visited her in Atlanta, GA, when she attended Emory University.

This trip was my first visit to see her in Nashville, TN, where she had moved to attend Meharry Medical College in August 1983. I had not yet told anyone outside of my family and my boss that the wedding was off or that I was pregnant. I had decided that I would rather share the news in person, so I told Mfon that I had something very important to share with her. When she met me at the airport in Nashville, and I walked out of the terminal wearing my maternity dungarees, she figured the pregnancy was the important news I wanted to share with her. I later informed her that not only was I pregnant but that the wedding had been called off or postponed indefinitely. She was immediately very supportive and sympathetic, and we agreed that the plan for my time in Nashville would be to relax, have a good time, and shop for the baby.

Mfon was a master planner. She had different fun activities planned for us to do during my visit. She took me on a tour of her new medical school and introduced me to her professors. She took me sightseeing in Nashville and arranged for us to go for a ride on the General Jackson Showboat, and we visited the Opryland Hotel. Then, to top it off, she organized a get-together and invited several of her new classmates to her apartment for a reception for her friend visiting from home. I was a little apprehensive about meeting several of Mfon's classmates at a get-together, as I was concerned that someone may ask me questions about myself or the baby that I may not want to answer. However, I did not want to be a party pooper, so I kept my apprehensions to myself.

Besides, the other reason Mfon had decided to hold the get-together that evening was because the 1984 Summer Olympics was being held in Los Angeles, CA, and the finals of the men's featherweight boxing competition was being held that night between Nigeria's Peter Konyegwachie and the United States' Meldrick Taylor. So Mfon's friends, both Nigerians and Americans, were going to watch the match together and cheer for their respective countries, so I helped Mfon prepare for the get-together. We got the apartment ready and fixed some finger foods, snacks, and drinks, and I told myself that hanging out with a group of boisterous medical students could not but cheer me up and keep me lighthearted. I felt further reassured as Mfon's guests arrived for the get-together; they were warm and friendly and treated me like an old friend. I had previously met a few of them during our tour of the Medical and Dental schools, but most of them I met for the first time, as Mfon introduced me as her best friend from back home.

We all chatted and got acquainted as we snacked and talked about the Olympic Games, which were going on right then, and anticipation mounted for the boxing finals between the USA and Nigeria starting within the hour. There were many animated discussions about which boxer would prevail and why. Both boxers had been undefeated and so were very well-matched, and the general consensus was that it would be a very close match and could go either way.

CHAPTER TWENTY-FIVE

The Flag-Waving American

Throughout the get-together, I was introduced to several of Mfon's classmates that evening and could not remember anyone's name, so I just smiled politely, made general conversation, and avoided referring to anyone by name. I was also relieved that most of the guests did not ask me many personal questions; a few asked if this was my first child, and some asked if I wanted a boy or a girl, and then we moved on to other topics and eventually to the Olympic Games. Everything was going well. That was until I was apprehended by the flag-waving American.

Remembering people's names is a skill that I am still striving to master to this day. So, when Mfon introduced me to this particular classmate, I did not remember his name afterward, but I remembered that she said they both met at an extracurricular activity held on campus for both dental and medical students.

The other reason I remembered him was because he welcomed me to "the great US of A" when we were introduced and would not stop at the usual social banter like everyone else. He proceeded to ply me with questions throughout the evening about the meaning of my name, as he had been told that all Nigerian names had meaning, to whether we were hoping for a boy or girl — until he finally asked me one of the dreaded questions.

He asked me what my husband did and how long we had been married. Those were questions I had hoped to avoid having to answer. I could not think of any way to evade or politely decline to answer the question, so I stated that he was a chemical engineer, and we were not married yet.

He promptly responded, "Are you going to marry him?"

The response/question was unexpected and caught me off guard, so I mumbled incoherently, "Of course," in a flustered voice before changing the subject back to the Olympics.

He then asked me if I had watched the Olympics' opening ceremony, and I answered that I had. He asked if I thought it was the greatest opening ceremony of any Olympics ever and that the "great ole US of A" knocked it out of the ballpark. I don't know which irritated me more, whether it was that he had asked me a personal question that I would rather not have answered or his 'flag-waving, proud to be an American' attitude, but I decided that I was not going to agree with his pompous declarations politely but would tell him what I really thought of the American Olympic opening ceremony.

So, I proceeded to inform him that I was in London on the day of the opening ceremony and that, interestingly enough, the British Broadcasting Corporation (BBC) had decided to air the Russian opening ceremony of the previous Olympics just before the 1984 American Olympic ceremony started so that the viewers could compare both opening ceremonies. I told him that I thought the Russian opening ceremony was much better than the American opening ceremony, which was also the consensus of the British viewers.

Wow, talk about waving a red cape in front of a bull!

"You really thought the Russian Olympic opening ceremony was better?" he exclaimed incredulously. "Are you serious or are you just pulling my leg?" he asked.

I proceeded to tell him smugly that it was not just my opinion but that the BBC conducted a poll after showing both events, and the poll confirmed that the majority of the British thought so, too.

"The Brits?" he laughed mockingly, "their opinions don't count around here anymore since we kicked them out with their 'taxation without representation' nonsense!"

After that comment, I thought it was time to get away from Yankee Doodle, so I politely excused myself as I saw Mfon waving for me to come and meet a newly arrived guest. I moved around the room, meeting and getting to know several more of Mfon's classmates until the boxing match between Nigeria and the USA started. Right before the match began, everybody found seats in front of the TV, and some people sat on the floor.

I found a comfortable seat in the corner, where I could watch the match but also leave the room unnoticed whenever I wanted. The truth was that while I was rooting for my countryman, Konyegwachie, to defeat the American and win Olympic gold for Nigeria, I was not a big boxing fan. I did not enjoy watching round after round of two men pounding each other to a pulp. I was only interested in seeing the beginning and the end of the match. So, to avoid interfering with the boxing enthusiasts' unbridled excitement, I sat in a corner seat in the back of the room.

To my surprise, Yankee Doodle, who I thought was so disgusted with me after my opening ceremony statement that I was sure he would have nothing more to say to me, came and sat beside me. He asked me if the seat next to me was free, sat in it, and resumed the conversation as if our Olympic opening ceremony argument had never occurred.

He started talking about music and telling me about different American groups he liked or had seen in concert. He then asked me what type of music I liked, and I responded that I liked jazz. He stated that he liked jazz too and asked if I knew that jazz was the only true Black American art form, as African Americans originated jazz. I could not believe my ears as I thought, here goes Yankee Doodle again, waving his American flag!

Once again, I felt I had to set him straight, so I calmly informed him that his statement was incorrect. I told him how I had recently read a historical piece that traced jazz's origin back to Africa. He was again incredulous at what he called my outrageous claim and attempted to educate me on the true origins of jazz, but I resolutely held on to my opinion.

The night ended with Meldrick Taylor, the American boxer, winning the Olympic gold medal on a controversial points decision over Peter Konyegwachie, the Nigerian favorite. Most of the Nigerians and some of the Americans thought that Konyegwachie got robbed and that Meldrick Taylor, the hometown favorite, got 'home cooking.' But not Yankee Doodle!

He thought and told everybody, very loudly, that the good ole US of A had pulled it out and narrowly won. Yankee Doodle was obstreperous in his jubilation, to the chagrin of the rest of us. Nevertheless, the get-together ended on a high note, and all had a good night.

CHAPTER TWENTY-SIX

Chance Meeting

I was heading back to Lagos a few days after the get-together at Mfon's house, so all her friends at the party wished me well and bid me farewell at the end of the party. The day before I was to leave Nashville, Mfon and I had been out running errands and picking up last-minute items. On the way back to her apartment, she remembered that she needed to pick up something from one of her classmates. She said we needed to swing by the Meharry Towers, where her classmate lived, for just a minute.

The towers were a high-rise apartment complex that housed some of the medical and dental students and also some of the medical school staff. We pulled into the parking lot and took the elevator to the floor Mfon's classmate lived on. We walked to his apartment and knocked for several minutes, but no one came to the door. She then tried the next apartment where another classmate lived, but he did not appear to be home either. So, we walked back to the elevator to head back to Mfon's apartment. While we were in the elevator, she suddenly had another bright idea and announced that we would stop by another classmate's apartment to see if he was home. We marched to the apartment, knocked on the door, and almost immediately, someone opened the door, and there, to my surprise, stood Yankee Doodle!

He looked equally surprised but pleased to see us and invited us in. Mfon explained that we had come to see another classmate, but he was not home, so she decided to stop by and check on him. We went into his apartment and visited for a few minutes before taking our leave and heading back to Mfon's apartment. My recollection of this visit was that it was a surprise. I left thinking the visit was pleasant, especially since Yankee Doodle and I did not get into any arguments during that visit.

The next day, I left Nashville, flew back to Lagos, and stepped back into the continuing saga that my life had become. I did not give a second thought to what I believed had been a chance, unplanned meeting with Yankee Doodle, but little did I know of its future, far-reaching implications.

CHAPTER TWENTY-SEVEN

Hope Springs Eternal

I returned home with numerous suitcases filled with baby items. I even shipped back a baby crib I had fallen in love with at Toys R Us in Nashville! I went back to work as I wanted to work till my due date so I could take my full three months of maternity leave after the baby arrived. I arrived home in Lagos in early August 1984, and the delivery due date my OB-GYN doctor gave me was September 30th, 1984, which was seven weeks away.

I spent the last few weeks getting ready for the baby's arrival while still going to work, and even though I only saw Tunde just once or twice after I returned, I was shocked at the suppressed excitement and anticipation I felt the first time I saw him again after my trip. I had not realized that somewhere deep inside my heart, I was still holding on to the hope or fairy tale that he was going to come sweeping in one day before the baby was born and declare that he wanted us to get married right away and be a family when our baby arrived. I guess hope springs eternal, but even that hope began to fade when, on his first visit after I returned from the USA, his only comment outside of small talk was to complain that he had not been informed before I left the country.

I marveled at the audacity of this man who had bailed on me and our child, had opted out of voting on whether to keep or abort our baby, had kowtowed to his mother's vociferous demands to abandon me and believed her well-orchestrated pantomime, put on to discredit me, now having the audacity to complain that I had not obtained his permission to travel out of the country. I swallowed several times as I choked back all the angry responses that swept across my mind and attempted to erupt out of my mouth. I decided to take my mother's advice to avoid arguments and conflict, keep the relationship cordial, hold my peace, and focus on staying peaceful to deliver a healthy baby.

So, I chose not to respond to his statements. As the date of the delivery drew closer, any lingering hope that he would somehow miraculously snap out of the spell he was under, come to his senses, and demand that we get married before our baby was born slowly but surely was dying. By mid-September, less than two weeks before my due date, cold, stark reality finally hit me in the face, like a douse of cold water, that this was going to be my reality. I was going to be an unwed mother; I was going to have to go through this experience of bringing a new life into the world alone as a single parent, without the love, support, and encouragement of the father of my child.

Unlike Cinderella, my story would not end with me riding off with my Prince into the sunset, but more like the hymn, Our God, Our Hope states, "They fly forgotten as a dream dies at the opening day." As my dream of reconciliation and marriage died, I knew, somewhere deep inside me, that anything left of our relationship had died also.

CHAPTER TWENTY-EIGHT

The Delivery

J ust as I planned, I went to work till Friday, September 28th, 1984, two days before my estimated due date of September 30th. Someone told me that most babies were not delivered on their estimated due dates, as those dates were usually guesstimations, and the babies were expected within a week or two of the due date. I had bought and read numerous baby books to prepare myself for this momentous event. I had read extensively about labor and delivery and studied all the symptoms of the onset of labor.

I had read all about Braxton Hicks contractions, also known as false labor, how to recognize true labor contractions, and how to time them. I had read so much literature and practiced all the suggested exercises and timing methods that I fancied myself somewhat of an expert and felt confident that I was ready. I had packed my little overnight suitcase to take to the hospital. I had packed all my brand new, cute baby outfits and my new mother-care nursing gowns and bras for myself. I had picked out the outfit I would wear to the hospital, and in my naivete, I had actually thought that I would drive myself to the hospital.

On the night of Saturday, September 29th, the day before my estimated due date, I was feeling drained, so I was lying in bed and watching an old movie on television after everyone had gone to bed. After a while, I started to feel some discomfort, so I adjusted my position, but then I began to feel a sharp pain in my abdomen, which I recognized as a mild contraction or maybe even a Braxton Hicks contraction. All my books had said not to be concerned since the first contractions were almost always false and not to rush to the hospital until the contractions were at least an hour to two hours apart, so I continued to watch the movie.

Sometime later, I heard my sister, Iyabo, go into the bathroom that adjoined my room. She heard the TV still on in my room and poked her head into it. As she asked me what I was watching, I felt another contraction, which caused me to breathe in sharply. When she expressed concern, I assured her it was probably a false contraction and that, according to my books, the real contractions would not start till morning. She was unconvinced by my theories and insisted on waking up our mother over my objections. My mother was also not impressed with my theories from my books and insisted that I get dressed immediately to leave for the hospital.

At this point, I was also beginning to lose confidence in my books and their theories as the contractions were closer together and stronger than anything they had described in all the books I had read. Also, I was very thankful that my younger sister, Olumide, had come home that weekend from her university and drove us all to the hospital. Contrary to my plan, I was not in any condition to drive a car, as I could barely stand after each contraction. Upon arrival at the maternity hospital, I was taken immediately to the delivery room as the contractions were now coming in quick succession, and the doctor was immediately paged.

I delivered a healthy, gorgeous baby boy within four hours of arriving at the clinic. When the doctor placed him in my arms, and I saw him for the first time, it was love at first sight. He looked so cute; his complexion reminded me of peaches and cream, and I cried as I thanked God for this wonderful, gorgeous gift. I knew that no matter what the future held or how hard the road ahead may be, I would always be grateful for this cuddly bundle of joy, my little 'Bobo,' born precisely on his estimated due date, September 30th, 1984, born on Sunday, just like me. I also knew, the minute I laid eyes on him, that he was going to go far, do great things and that he was going to be a leader.

CHAPTER TWENTY-NINE

The Naming Ceremony

We were discharged from the hospital after three days and went home to a warm welcome from my family. In Nigerian Yoruba culture, of which we were both a part, a baby boy was named on the 9th day after his birth. The naming ceremony usually took place at the home of the paternal grandfather or the home of the baby's father. At the naming ceremony, the baby's names are announced for the first time.

Tunde informed me that he wanted the naming ceremony to be at his house and that his father would be coming from out of town for the ceremony, and his mother, stepfather, and siblings would all be in attendance. My initial reaction was to refuse to take my baby to his house for his family to perform the naming ceremony, but again, my mother's counsel not to make decisions out of my hurt and anger prevailed, and I agreed to the arrangement. However, in the days leading to the naming ceremony, my trepidation and anxiety grew at the prospect of taking my son to be named in a house that should have been his home with both of his parents. Also, the ceremony would be officiated by people who did not mean me well and were adversarial to my well-being. The thought of seeing Tunde's mother again for the first time since the Witch Doctor saga made me almost break out in hives.

On the morning of the ceremony, after prayers had been offered at our house, I left for Tunde's house with the baby, accompanied by my sisters-in-law and some cousins. My mother and older siblings opted to wait at our house, having previously decided not to attend the ceremony at Tunde's house due to his family's total disregard for etiquette and respectful protocol concerning my family. This trip was also my first visit to Tunde's new apartment, which was supposed to have been our new home together. Our small delegation went in and said our polite hellos to his family members and his mother. I sat straight-faced through the ceremony, struggling to fight back my tears.

As soon as the official naming ceremony was over, Tunde's side was shocked when we got up to leave, as they had erroneously assumed that the baby and I would spend the day there and be part of the rest of the festivities they had planned. We declined politely, excused ourselves, and headed towards our vehicles. Tunde was obviously distraught as he explained to me that the caterers were en route to deliver the food, and several of his family and friends were also coming later in the day and were expecting to see the baby. I reminded him all I had agreed to do was attend the naming ceremony, not partake in a whole-day celebration. We got into our waiting vehicles and left. My sister-in-law commented on how ironic it was that the same people who had plotted and opposed our marriage plans and failed to acknowledge me and my son or my family now wanted us to stay and socialize with them all day. I wryly smiled as I responded that it was not me or my accompanying family members they were interested in. No, they wanted the baby to be present and on display when their other family members and friends arrived. One of his family members had even asked why we couldn't leave the baby behind if we chose not to stay. We informed them that the seven-day-old baby was on breast milk and needed to be with his mother.

As we drove back to my family's home, I thought and reflected on the naming ceremony that just took place. Tunde's father gave the three main names, and his mother chose not to add any additional names. The norm or tradition was that the baby went by the name pronounced by the grandfather or the grandmother. After what I had gone through with his family and the fact that he made it my choice whether to keep or abort the baby, I decided that I was going to give my baby a name that was both meaningful and also reflected his story and mine. After much reflection, soul searching, and prayer, I believe the name given to me was divinely inspired and appropriate.

I named him "Babasijibomi," which means, "God has surrounded me with his protection." I felt very strongly that God himself had protected and brought my son and me through the darkness of fear and despair, false accusations, rejection, abandonment, and hopelessness as He surrounded us both with His protection and love.

CHAPTER THIRTY

Mad at God

In Nigerian culture, the birth of a child is always a joyous celebration, so from the day the mother and child return home, family and friends come by to visit and express their congratulations. They also bring food and gifts for the mother and baby.

The first month after returning home was euphoric. My mother and other family members cared for the baby, bathing him and changing his diapers. They would only bring him to me when it was time to breastfeed him, insisting that I rest and allow my body to heal and eat the nutritious meals that had been prepared at the house, in addition to all the meals brought over by friends and family. With all the family and friends coming in and out to greet the baby and me, the atmosphere was very festive, keeping my spirit high.

Add to this the fact that my birthday that year fell on a Sunday, two weeks after my son was born on a Sunday. This fact was even more remarkable to me because I was born on a Sunday and now gave birth to my first child on a Sunday in the year when my birthday again fell on a Sunday. I felt like there was some hidden significance about all this, which would hopefully be revealed to us sometime in the future.

At least, according to the famous English nursery rhyme titled, "Monday's child is fair of face," we know that "the child that is born on the Sabbath day is bonny and blight and good and gay." I learned later that "bonny" means pleasing to the eye, pretty or handsome, and blight means joyous, merry, glad, and cheerful. I felt happy that my son and I were born on the best day of all, according to the authoritative nursery rhyme!

After the guests and well-wishers had come and gone, we settled into a routine. It was just the baby and me at home, and some of the dark clouds started attempting to return. There were reminders that I was a single parent and an unwed mother. The eye-opening realization that I could no longer come and go as I pleased but now had the responsibility, without the help of a husband, for another human life. With this realization and the weight of responsibility came resentment and anger.

I began to feel angry at God. I thought He had singled me out to make me an example and punish me for breaking my vow to Him. After all, I knew several other friends were also having relations with their boyfriends, and they had not gotten pregnant. The more these thoughts ran through my mind, the darker and thicker the clouds became, and the madder I got at God. *How could He treat me so badly? How could He allow me to end up in this lonely, forlorn place with all my hopes and dreams dashed? How could He let my hopes for a beautiful, dream wedding, a romantic honeymoon, my new home with my husband, and the pretty nursery where I would have welcomed my first child come to nothing? How could He allow Tunde's mother to succeed in her lying, evil scheme against me? How could He allow me to end up alone, unmarried, rejected, and abandoned, still living in my parents' house and raising my son alone? Why was He treating me like I was the vilest and worst sinner ever born and making me a public spectacle?*

As the voices taunted me, I got madder and madder at God, concluding that He was neither fair nor loving and that I would no longer waste my time speaking to Him anymore. That's right. No more prayers and no more reading the Bible. *What good had it done me thus far?* Henceforth, I was no longer on speaking terms with God.

CHAPTER THIRTY-ONE

Owning Up

I felt justified in my actions; after all, I reasoned that God had let me down. He had singled me out, had not looked out for me, and had let evil forces overcome me. What good had all my prayers and Bible reading done me until then? I felt sure that people who did not pray or waste their time reading the Bible got better outcomes than I did. There was no reason to waste my time if He would let these things happen to me! I was done with God and reasoned I had every right to be.

As the days turned into weeks, my feelings of self-justification and indignation started fading away, and I began to feel self-doubt and sorrow. I was in a dark, lonely place and felt lost and afraid. As I tried to sort through this new feeling of sorrow, loneliness, and self-doubt, all my excuses and blame started falling down like dominoes. The voice of truth in my head asked me, "Who really let me down? Who had allowed this to happen to me? Who was responsible for the situation in which I found myself?" I could no longer lie to myself and had to own up and take responsibility for my actions. I had to admit

I had let myself down and was solely responsible for my present situation. The period of being mad at God and not speaking with Him lasted about one month, from the end of October to the end of November 1984. That was the longest, darkest, and loneliest month of my life. I did not realize that hope and joy would also depart after I abandoned my prayer and Bible reading time.

The darkness was darker than any I had ever experienced in my life, and worst of all, I missed my time with Him so badly that it shocked me. After I admitted to myself and confessed to God that my present predicament was a result of all my bad choices and nobody else's fault, amazingly, the darkness lifted, and I began to feel hope again. The truth was that I should have known better because I had been raised in a Christian home.

My father was a local preacher in the Methodist church, and we grew up with the tradition of holding family devotionals every morning in our home, led by my father. I knew what the Word of God said about sex before marriage, but I still flirted and played with sin till I got caught. I had subscribed to the partial obedience school of my generation, the "God understands" lying, demonic philosophy.

The other part was that I could not wholly blame Tunde for the mess I had gotten myself into. He had never subscribed to the abstinence rule or ever confessed anything more than a social belief in God. He certainly did not have a similar upbringing to mine, nor a tradition of family prayer and Bible reading time while growing up. I had not realized how important it was to choose a life partner who not only knew and loved God but would make decisions for our future family based on God's word.

Anyhow, after I broke my self-imposed embargo on communing with God and reading my Bible, the clouds of sadness and depression that had enshrouded me began to lift. Joy and hope returned, along with laughter and anticipation.

I could now sing along with Johnny Nash. I truly could see clearly. Everything that blocked my view was finally gone. All of the darkness had left me, leaving me standing in the bright sunshine. It was truly amazing that I could see more clearly after I admitted and confessed my faults.

I learned that I could not move forward until and unless I admitted my own fault and took responsibility for my actions. I could see, more practically through my own experience, the lesson from the Bible when the Prophet Samuel confronted King Saul with his sin of disobedience; Saul immediately made excuses and blamed the people for his actions.

In contrast, when confronted with his sin with Bathsheba, David immediately owned up to his sin and declared that he had sinned before the Lord. Saul never took responsibility for his sins and acts of omission and thereby lost both his life and the kingdom, while David was quick to confess his sins and ask forgiveness, thereby receiving mercy and restoration. This explains why God could use and bless David but rejected Saul. I certainly did not want to end up like Saul.

CHAPTER THIRTY-TWO

The Rainbow

The one thing that became clear to me after coming out of that awful stretch of darkness that developed after I cut communication with God was that I needed to know more of Him than I did. This step was essential in order to move on successfully from where I was because I never again in my life wanted to go through the pain and darkness I had just gone through.

The next day, after my relationship with the Lord was restored, a friend came by to visit me. Bunmi and I had gone to law school together and shared an apartment in Ibadan, Nigeria, during our National Youth Service Corp a few years before. I shared with her what had been going on in my life, including my reconnection and newfound closeness with God. She then told me she had given her life to the Lord a few weeks ago. She had been invited to attend a Bible study held at a school in Ebute Metta, Lagos, hosted by a group called The Prayer Band. She shared that she had given her life to the Lord and become born again.

I was surprised because she had been a social Christian like me, and we both thought that the "born again" people were fanatics, but I could see, as she shared with me, that there was something different about her. So, when she invited me to attend the same Bible study the following week, I accepted her invitation. Deep inside me, I knew I needed something more, but I was unsure what it was. I thought perhaps it was a more in-depth knowledge of the Bible, but after listening to Bunmi's testimony, I felt I could find it in this Bible study.

So, on Wednesday, December 5th, 1984, I left my son at home with my mother and drove to Ebute Metta to the Saint Jude Anglican Church and School. The Bible study was being held in one of the school's classrooms. Bunmi had assured me that she would be there, so when I walked into the classroom, I was expecting to see her, but she was not there, and I did not know any of the people who were there that night.

As I hesitated at the entrance, trying to decide if I should go back outside to wait for Bunmi or walk alone into this classroom full of strangers, an older gentleman approached me and offered to escort me to a seat. I asked him if this was the Prayer Band Bible study group, and when he answered affirmatively, I told him I was invited by my friend Bunmi, who wasn't there yet. The gentleman suggested that I come in and enjoy the Bible Study until my friend arrived, so I followed him to the seat he led me to and sat down.

The Bible study was just about to get started. They opened with a prayer, and then everybody sang several choruses, acapella, clapping in rhythm. There were no musical instruments, but the choruses were sung with such passion, gusto, and reverence that I felt like the singing was not to entertain or pass the time. It felt like an offering being offered up to God.

After the choruses, a young man, who looked not much older than me, walked up to the front, prayed, and shared a message on the similarities between Joseph and Jesus. He went through several Bible passages showing how God had worked in both lives and their relationship with God. He spoke on how God used Joseph to save all the nations of the world from famine and destruction as a foreshadowing of Jesus coming to die on the cross to save all mankind from sin and separation from God.

I had never heard the Bible preached like that ever before or understood it quite so clearly. It was like a light was turned on in my heart and mind, and I knew I needed what Joseph and Jesus had: an intimate relationship with God. When he made the altar call at the end of his message, I went forward without any hesitation. I received Jesus as my Lord and Savior at that moment, and I became born again!

CHAPTER THIRTY-THREE

A Giddy Joy

On the night of December 5th, 1984, I gave my life to the Lord, confessed Jesus as my Lord and Savior, and was born again. The first emotion I remember was this feeling of peace that came all over me as if a burden had been lifted off me and all was well. I had this peaceful feeling that everything would be alright, even though I didn't know how.

The other emotion that I remember was this giddy joy that was hard to explain, that infused my whole being. After they had prayed for those of us who came forward to give our lives to Jesus that night, someone instructed me to tell all my family and friends what had just happened to me. They then instructed me on the importance of having a personal quiet time with the Lord every day and suggested Bible passages to read first and devotional aids to use.

I drove back home that night a different person from who I was when I left. I walked into the house and announced to my mother and sister that I was now born again, as I had given my life to Jesus and asked Him to be my Lord and Savior. My mother said that was what I did when I went through the confirmation process at our church, that we had always prayed to God through Jesus and that He was already our Lord. My sister was also very skeptical of this newfound fervor.

I tried unsuccessfully to explain to my mother and sister what the difference was, but I could tell that they felt that this newfound faith was a result of my present circumstances. I agreed that it was my present circumstances that made me realize that I did not have the intimate relationship that resulted in salvation and led me to discover the difference between being a church member and being a born-again believer in Jesus.

The other thing that changed for me immediately was that I began to hunger for the Word of God and the things of God. The Word of God took on a new life and excitement, and all the stories I had read or heard since my youth came alive in a new way. The Word of God truly became flesh and came alive in my life. I started to attend The Prayer Band and Bible study regularly every Wednesday and enjoy fellowship with other born-again believers.

There was one member of my family, my brother, that I was looking forward to sharing my newfound faith with because I knew he would understand and affirm it. I remember the day I shared it with him; we were at my mother's shop on Moore Road, Lagos, Nigeria. When I told him I was born again and shared my testimony with him, he immediately said, "Praise the Lord!" He then shared 1 Peter 2:2 (KJV) with me, *"As newborn babes, desire the sincere milk of the word that you may grow thereby."* He was very happy for me and prayed with me before he left. I knew that my brother, Wole, would understand and be glad for me because he had announced to the family several years before when he was still a student at the University of Ife, Nigeria, that he had become born again.

As I grew in the Lord, I felt increasingly that the Lord wanted me to share my testimony, particularly with my family, friends, and colleagues. So, feeling that I should not keep this newfound joy and good news to myself, I embarked on a quest to share my testimony face-to-face with all my friends.

At this time, early to mid-1985, most of my friends were married, had started families, and were all aware of what had happened to me. So, when I paid them each a visit, took out my Bible, and shared my testimony and the salvation message with them, they were understandably taken aback and amused at my newfound zeal. They all laughed that I had become one of those fanatics we all used to laugh at on the university campus. Some advised me not to let the fact that I was now an unwed mother turn me into a fanatic, while others offered to introduce me to some eligible, possible dates.

I was so happy and excited about my newfound faith that I chose not to take offense but continue to grow in the Lord and just pray for my friends. I felt that the only way to convince them was to let them see the difference in my life as I grew in the Lord. In the meantime, I made new friends among the born-again believers I was meeting at The Prayer Band Bible study. I also started to attend an evangelical church that preached about being born again and being baptized with the Holy Spirit with the evidence of speaking in other tongues.

CHAPTER THIRTY-FOUR

The Visit

Meanwhile, it became apparent that Tunde really believed that after the baby was a few months old and things had settled down, we would just pick up where we had left off. He stopped by the house one evening, and while leading him to the sitting room, he asked why he could not visit with the baby in my bedroom. When I stated that I would prefer the visits be confined to the sitting room, he asked me, in a scoffing tone, how long I intended to keep up the hostilities. On another visit, he suggested that we all go for a drive together, and when I declined, he appeared miffed and left shortly after.

Several days later, I received a surprise visit from one of his close friends, who was also an attorney. The visit was a surprise for several reasons. The first reason was that this friend lived and practiced in Ibadan, the city where Bunmi and I had lived during our National Youth Service Corp. Ibadan was at least a one-and-a-half to two-hour drive from my family's home in Ilaje, Bariga in Lagos. The second reason was that I had not seen this friend in almost two years, and the third reason was that he had never visited my home before this time. He acknowledged that he realized that his visit would be a surprise to me but that he came into town for a legal matter and afterward visited Tunde. He said he then decided to seize the opportunity to stop by to see me and the baby before heading back out of town.

During the visit, Tunde's friend informed me that Tunde told him that I was rebuffing all his attempts to mend fences between us and that I would not spend time with him or allow him to get anywhere close to me. He asked me what I hoped to achieve by my actions and that if I chased Tunde off, who else did I think would marry me now that I was a single mother? He proceeded to tell me that no young single man would ever marry me since I had a child by another man and that my only options would be to hook up with either a divorcee or a widower who already had children of their own also and would not be opposed to marrying a single mother, to help them raise their kids.

I was speechless with shock and indignation. However, Tunde's friend had not run out of words. His advice to me was to swallow my pride, cease the hostilities, and warmly receive and welcome Tunde back while I still had a chance and stop putting on airs and acting as if I was still a single young lady with a lot of options. Even though his words cut through me like a cruel stab to the heart, I willed myself not to react but maintained my composure and a stiff upper lip as I asked him if he was done or if there was anything else he had to say. Sheepishly, he said he was only trying to get me to face the harsh realities of my circumstances, come to my senses, and act accordingly. I thanked him for his visit and wished him a safe trip back to Ibadan.

As I watched his car drive out through the gates of my father's house, a multitude of emotions were washing over me like waves. I felt everything from hurt and resentment to shame and sorrow, anger, fear and uncertainty, self-doubt, to sheer amazement at his audacity, his rude, disrespectful, and impudent tone and choice of words. He had obviously come to put me in my place and cut me down to size, and as I stood there trembling, watching his taillight disappear, I felt as if he had succeeded in his mission. I went into my room, locked the door, and sat down as I replayed over and over in my mind the words that Tunde's friend had just spoken to me.

The more I replayed it, the more it sounded like truth, and the more I shrunk in my seat, feeling smaller and smaller. Then those old voices in my head joined in and gleefully jumped on the bandwagon, telling me I would end up an old maid, alone and unloved. The voices kept telling me that nobody else would want me or love me now and that I would never achieve my dreams. I burst into tears and sat there trembling as tears ran down my cheeks, tears of hurt and humiliation, cringing at how small he had made me feel. I fell on my knees, in tears, and started to pray, at first just asking God to take away the hurt and the humiliation, the fear and doubt that was attempting to overwhelm me.

Suddenly, holy indignation came upon me and went all over me as I remembered who I was; I was a new creature in Christ Jesus; I had authority and power and could ask what I wanted of my Father. So, I began to pray with passion, clarity, and specificity and told God that because of what Tunde's friend had said to me, I wanted God to confound the heathen and show them that He was my God and that I was His child.

I asked God to give me the exact husband that Tunde's friend had said that I could never have: a young man who is not a divorcee or a widower, a young man who has never been married, has no children, and who would love me above every other woman on the face of the earth, and would accept my son as his firstborn child. I asked God to bring me a professional man like I had always dreamed of, give me the dream wedding I had always wanted, and do it all in the presence of my enemies. I also asked that because of the way that Tunde's mother had rejected me, treated me with hatred and contempt, and lied against me, I asked God to give me a mother-in-law who would love me like her own daughter, and we would have a very close relationship.

By the time I finished my impassioned prayer, the tears had stopped, the fears and hurts were gone, and I rose to my feet with renewed joy and expectation. The enemies' attempt to intimidate and cower me had failed, and what the enemy had meant for evil, God had turned it around for my good. Tunde's friend had inadvertently helped me to define with specificity what type of man I wanted as my future husband and to articulate it with clarity to my Father God.

In fact, his hurtful remarks had caused me to upgrade my terms and conditions so that when it happened, when the answer manifested, there would be no doubt in anyone's mind that this was indeed the doing of the Lord. In retrospect, I almost want to thank Tunde's friend for being instrumental in changing the trajectory of my prayer and, thereby, also the trajectory of my life.

CHAPTER THIRTY-FIVE

Camp Meeting

I returned to work at the law firm in January of 1985, after my 90 days of maternity leave, with a new fire in my eyes and a new zeal in my heart. I had prayed and asked God to create openings for me to share my new life-changing faith with my colleagues at the law firm. After the experience with my law school friends and their spouses, when I tried to share my faith with them, I learned to slow down, pray for God's leading, and wait for opportunities or appropriate openings.

It had become apparent to me that most of my friends and some of my family members considered my newfound born-again salvation and zeal as somewhat similar to a jailhouse or prison salvation! Like the saying that there is no atheist in a foxhole, they probably thought that my new religious zeal was simply a coping mechanism possibly resulting from the traumatic events that led to my becoming an unwed mother.

I started attending Sunday services at a new charismatic church started by a young medical doctor who had also become born again and was teaching and preaching the exciting, life-changing, born-again relationship with Jesus I had experienced. The praise and worship was joyful, exuberant, and worshipful, and the message was exciting and insightful. My sister, Iyabo, finally decided to attend the service with me one Sunday after several weeks of me telling her how great the service was and how rich the Word of God was being preached. She also saw the changes in my personality and priorities and wanted to know more.

One Sunday, they announced that registration was open for the trip to attend Kenneth Hagin's Camp Meeting in Tulsa, OK, that summer. I immediately got excited and decided to register to attend the camp meeting with the church group because Kenneth Hagin had become my favorite prophet and minister. I was introduced to his books and tapes right after being saved, and I loved the simplicity, power, and authority with which he preached. His teaching on the Authority of the Believer changed my life and played a significant part in changing the trajectory of my prayers. I convinced my sister Iyabo to register for the trip also, and in July 1985, we attended the Kenneth Hagin Camp Meeting in Tulsa, OK, as part of the group from Christ Church, Lagos, Nigeria.

It was so exciting to be part of the great multitude of believers from all over the world attending the conference. The lineup of speakers was like the Who's Who of charismatic ministers: Frederick K.C. Price and his wife Betty, Kenneth Copeland and his wife Gloria, and several other prominent ministers, but the one I was most excited about hearing preach live and in person, was Papa Hagin. There was something about his spirit and the anointing upon his life that touched me like no other preacher I listened to.

I experienced my first rude awakening as a Charismatic Christian on this trip. I found out that not all born-again Christians were excited about the Word or had put aside their past deceptive or fleshly lifestyles. I was shocked when one of the brothers on the trip, who had appeared or seemed to be such a strong Christian, invited me to join a group of other brethren for a "midnight swim" one day after the camp meeting session. I thought it would be apparent to anyone with any common sense that no spiritual good could come from a group of single Christian adults indulging in a midnight swim together.

Predictably, several of the midnight swimmers did not make it to the camp meeting sessions the next day, and some of them left the group under a cloud shortly after. Indeed, there were wolves in disguise among the sheep, but that made me more determined to grow even closer to God than ever before, as I already had my watershed experience and would not let the devil trip me up ever again.

One of my great desires was to attend a charismatic church service when my sister and I went to Nashville, TN, after the camp meeting. So, I mentioned to God while praying that I would love to attend a charismatic church service while I was in Nashville. The next day at the camp meeting was called an All Nations Day, and we were all requested to come dressed in our traditional attires, representing our various countries. So, we proudly donned our colorful Nigerian outfits and joined the thousands of other believers from all over the world, celebrating the All Nations Day.

During the lunch break that day, a group of us were sitting outside the auditorium when some ladies walked up to us and asked what country we were from. They expressed their admiration for our outfits and how exciting meeting believers from various countries was. Then, one of the ladies asked us if we were going straight back home to our country after the conference. Several people in the group responded "yes" to her inquiry, but I answered that my sister and I were going to Nashville, TN, after the conference for a couple of weeks before going home. She turned to me in surprise and exclaimed that she was from Nashville, TN. I jumped up and announced excitedly to her that she was an answer to prayer, as I had just asked the Lord for a believer to invite me to church in Nashville.

The lady said she would be glad to invite me, but she was going to New York City from Tulsa to visit her sister and, therefore, would not be attending her church until the Sunday following her return. She introduced herself as Anita and offered to give me her pastor's telephone number. She said he would gladly welcome me, so we exchanged information, and I gave her my friend Mfon's telephone number and address. When I handed her the sheet of paper with my friend's information, she exclaimed in surprise that her friend and fellow church member lived on the same street as my friend Mfon and would gladly give us a ride to church on that Sunday. So, she gave me her friend's telephone number and address and promised to call me when she returned to Nashville.

I was ecstatic at how quickly God had answered my prayer and the precise and exact manner in which He had done it. When we arrived in Nashville, as soon as we had settled in at my friend's apartment, I called Anita's friend, Darlene, to introduce myself and to ask her if we could go to church with her that Sunday. She was not home, so I left my name and number and a message for her to call me back.

Shortly afterward, there was a knock on the door, and I wondered who it could be since my friend had not indicated that she was expecting anyone when she dropped us at the apartment. I looked through the peephole, and to my surprise, I saw Yankee Doodle standing there, smiling broadly. I opened the door, and after exchanging greetings, I informed him that my friend Mfon was not home, to which he responded that he had not come to see my friend but to welcome me. Taken aback, I asked how he knew that I was in town, and he responded that Mfon had told him that I was coming back, and when he heard that I had arrived, he came by to welcome me back.

I was floored and touched that he had actually driven all the way down to Mfon's apartment to welcome me and say hello. So, we sat down and visited for a while. He asked me if I had any new jazz favorites since my last visit. I laughed and told him that I was not into jazz anymore but was now a big gospel music fan. I informed him that my sister Iyabo and I had just come to Nashville from attending Kenneth Hagin's Camp Meeting in Tulsa, OK, and that it was the greatest conference and concert I had ever attended. We shared some highlights from our fantastic camp meeting experience. When he finally got a word in, he mentioned that I was different from how I was at my last visit.

Perceiving this as an opportunity to share my testimony, I announced to him that I had given my life to Jesus and been born again. I asked him if he knew what that meant. He laughed incredulously and retorted that, of course, he knew what that meant. I apologized, stating that I had not meant to insult his intelligence but had been asked what that meant on several occasions. He then shared that he had given his life and become born again when he was in high school but had fallen away since then. He visited for a little longer before taking his leave, promising to call or stop by again soon.

The next day, Anita's friend Darlene called me back, and after I introduced myself and asked if my sister and I could attend church with her, she immediately said yes and asked for the address where she should pick us up. When I gave her the address, she laughed and said that we were just up the street from her, that she would be right over, and hung up the phone. Within five minutes, Darlene knocked on the door, came in, hugged us like long-lost friends, and stayed for a long time, just talking and getting to know us. That Sunday, she picked us up for church and introduced us to her husband, three sons, pastor, and several other church members. The service was every bit as enjoyable and fulfilling as I had hoped that it would be. After service, she dropped us off after arranging to pick us up the next day to go shopping.

CHAPTER THIRTY-SIX

New Friendships

D arlene invited us to a Bible study at her house that Wednesday evening and introduced us to the other families in their Bible study group as her new Christian friends from Nigeria. We were surprised to discover that one of the couples had also just returned from camp meeting, and we excitedly compared notes on our favorite speakers and singers from the camp meeting. We went back to church with Darlene the following Sunday and attended the Bible study at her home the following Wednesday. By this time, Anita was back in town and was at the church service, and she informed us that she would probably also see us at the Bible study on Wednesday at Darlene's house.

Also, at this time, Yankee Doodle, now known as Jeffrey, had become a friend, as he had called and checked on my sister and me several times and had also given us rides to the store. So, I invited him to Darlene's Bible study, stating that it would be highly beneficial for him on his Christian journey to meet and fellowship with other born-again

Christians who were excited about Jesus. Also, after our last conversation, he said that he had felt impressed in his heart that he needed to re-dedicate his life to the Lord and had done so in his apartment, hence my eagerness to introduce him to other believers who could continue to encourage him in his renewed faith.

After the Bible study, I introduced Jeffrey to Anita, and while we stood there talking, they realized that they knew each other as Anita worked at Meharry Medical College, where Jeffrey was a student. As the three of us stood outside Darlene's house talking, I had what I thought was a great idea to facilitate a hook-up between Anita and Jeffrey. In my mind, it would be ideal because they were African American, lived in Nashville, were affiliated with Meharry Medical College, were Christians, knew some of the same people, and looked great together! Moreover, she could encourage him in his faith, and what better way to thank and honor the person that the Lord had used to answer my prayer at camp meeting?

The more I thought about it, the more inspired and selfless the idea appeared to be, so I announced that I needed to go back inside to check on my sister, but I said that they should continue their conversation and exchange contact information. I went back into Darlene's house thinking that once left alone, the conversation between the two of them would blossom, and a relationship would ensue. That thought did not last very long.

Within minutes, Jeffrey followed me back inside the house, confronted me, and asked me what I was trying to do. I feigned innocence, pretending to look puzzled by his question, but he wasn't buying it. Jeffrey accused me of trying to pawn him off on Anita and that I was not so slick as he was on to me. So, I sheepishly admitted that I had hoped he and Anita would hit it off as they seemed like such a good match. He looked me straight in the eye and told me that he was not interested in Anita. He was only interested in me and would appreciate it if I did not try to pass him off to Anita or anyone else in the future.

Even though Jeffrey had expressed his interest in me on one of his subsequent visits to see me at my friend's apartment, I had not taken him seriously and had dismissed it as a mere passing fancy, mainly as he had just recently re-dedicated his life to the Lord. I told him that his focus should be on developing his relationship with the Lord and getting closer to God, and then later, he could ask God to show him who his wife was. Secondly, I was not in the least interested in getting involved in another long-distance relationship. Finally, and most importantly, I felt sure, particularly after my impassioned prayer back home concerning my spouse, that God's choice for me would be a strong Western Nigerian Christian brother. After all, I was from Western Nigeria and had dated predominantly Western Nigerian guys.

So, while I felt flattered by Jeffrey's interest in me, I told him there could be nothing more than friendship between us. I thought that after the incident at the Bible study, I had dissuaded him, but on the contrary, he stopped by to visit a couple of days later as if nothing had happened.

Each time he visited, he would ask many questions about Nigeria and what was involved in the marriage process, insisting that he was just curious.

He was so persistent and obvious in his admiration that Darlene started kidding me and joking that my "just a friend" appeared to want to be more. I maintained that it was just a passing fancy and that he would get over it once I returned to Nigeria.

To my surprise, Jeffrey proved me wrong when shortly after my sister and I returned home, he called me on the telephone to inform me that not only had his feelings not changed, but he was also even more sure I was the one for him. He then started calling me every month and sending me letters and cards expressing his affection. I was surprised at his persistence and even more surprised at his regular phone calls because, in 1985, international calls were very expensive. I began to wonder if he could possibly be the one, but I could not shake my conviction that the husband God would provide for me would be a Nigerian believer.

CHAPTER THIRTY-SEVEN

The Deciding Factor

L ater that year, I attended a Christian conference in Ede, Western Nigeria, hosted by a prophet called Papa Elton. The prophetic conference theme was, "Gather my people together who have made a covenant with me by sacrifice." Papa Elton was a British missionary who had mentored many early Nigerian evangelical Christian leaders and was a renowned Apostle and Prophet. At this conference, Papa Elton prophesied that Africa and Africans would be at the forefront of God's end-time move and go from being considered 'third world' and last to being first and leading the world. At the end of the conference, I had concluded that with all the exciting things that had been prophesied that God was going to do in Africa and with Africans, He could not possibly be leading me to get involved with an American and miss out on the great move that was coming.

On the last day before we left Ede, I had the opportunity to consult with one of the speakers at the conference, Brother Emeka. I told him about my American suitor and how I was beginning to think that it might be the enemy's ploy to sideline me and take me out of God's will. He counseled me that the prophecy included all Africans and not just those residing on the continent of Africa and that I should continue to pray and seek the Lord's face about the relationship. After that, I began to pray earnestly, asking the Lord to show me if Jeffrey was indeed his choice for me.

Meanwhile, Jeffrey continued to call me regularly despite his telephone getting disconnected numerous times after he ran up his bill. He also started sending me letters addressed to Mrs. Jola Olufon Moore, much to the consternation of my mother, who wondered if I was hiding anything from her. When I told Jeffrey to stop sending me such letters as he was alarming my mother, he refused and told me that he was exercising his faith by "calling those things which be not, as though they were." I could not admonish him further after that.

On one of his telephone calls, Jeffrey asked me what I would like for Christmas, and I replied without hesitation that I would love to receive an Amplified Bible. He promised to see what he could do to get it to me by Christmas. To my surprise, Jeffrey discovered that one of Mfon's friends was coming home to Lagos, Nigeria, for Christmas. So, Jeffrey gave the friend the Amplified Bible to give to me, and I got it before Christmas, just as he had promised.

Apart from his tenacity and persistence, this was my first tangible sign that he might be "the one." The second sign was when I telephoned him, just after Christmas, to thank him for my Christmas present. Jeffrey had gone to his parents' home in Flint, MI, for the holidays and was excited to hear from me and was happy to hear that I received my Amplified Bible before Christmas. He then suddenly asked me if I would like to meet his parents. Surprised by the question, I asked him what I would say to them, and he responded that I should just say hello and introduce myself.

Before I could decline, Jeffrey handed the phone to his mother, who, in a cheery voice, said, "Hello, this is Dolores Moore. How are you?"

I was taken aback and surprised as I had never had any friend's mother introduce themselves to me by their first name. She went on to ask after my family and ended the conversation by inviting me to visit them in Flint, MI, the next time I was in the United States. His father also came on the phone, introduced himself as Bill Moore, and chatted with me for a few minutes. When Jeffrey returned on the line, he laughingly told me that his parents had officially invited me without his prompting. I had to visit his family on my next trip. I again felt in my spirit that God was confirming his choice.

By the summer of 1986, when I went back to Nashville, it was official that we were dating. Jeffrey met me at the airport and drove me to Darlene's house. Mfon was on a rotation out of town, so Darlene had offered to host me at her home. She found it hilarious that I was finally admitting what she had known from the very beginning, that Jeffrey and I were not "just friends." I was nervous about our upcoming trip to Flint, MI, to visit his family. I was concerned that they might not like the gifts I had brought for them from Nigeria or think that the gift was a bribe and that maybe I should not present the gifts. Jeffrey kept reassuring me that they would love me and appreciate the gifts that I had brought for them. All I could do was hope he was right. I readied myself for the encounter, silencing the voice that tried to bring doubt and fear. Fortunately, the voice was forced into submission when I finally met his family. The visit was wonderful. Jeffrey's parents, as were his brothers and sisters, were even warmer and friendlier in person.

At the end of the visit, as we headed back to Nashville, I knew without a shadow of a doubt that Jeffrey was God's choice for me, and he was the exact answer to all the requests I had made to God. Jeffrey was single, never married, not a widower or a divorcee, had no children, and had already accepted my son as his own, and his parents already loved and accepted both me and my son. In addition, his love and affection for me had grown even greater over the past year when we last saw each other, and the best part of it all was that his love and passion for God had grown greater also.

I realized that God had not just given me a man with a professional qualification as I had requested; Jeffrey was a medical doctor, the son of a medical doctor, and the sibling of two medical doctors. I felt confident that God had thrown in the medical doctor bonus to make my father in heaven happy and at my father's request to Him! Jeffrey and my friend Mfon were scheduled to graduate the following year, 1987, from medical and dental school, respectively, and I planned to be in attendance at their graduation to cheer them on.

When we got back from the trip to Flint, MI, to meet his family, we started talking in earnest about when and where we would get married. Jeffrey said that if we got married in the United States, we could do it sooner, and we would not have to continue to be apart from each other. I reminded him that in Nigerian culture, the wedding was not just between the couple but also between their families and that all my family were in Nigeria. Furthermore, I was prepared to wait as long as it took to have the dream wedding I had prayed for. I would not compromise this time, and Jeffrey supported my decision.

So, I went back to Nashville, TN, in May of 1987 and cheered happily as my best friend, Mfon, and my fiancée, Jeffrey, graduated from Meharry Medical and Dental School. Jeffrey and I officially got engaged after the graduation, and Jeffrey gave me his medical school graduation ring to put on until he could afford to buy me an engagement ring. We decided that we would get married the following year, the summer of 1988, after he would have started his residency program and would be better able to support a wife and child.

CHAPTER THIRTY-EIGHT

Amazing Miracle

L ike a miracle unfolding and coming to pass before my eyes, three years from the period of my deepest hurt, rejection, and pain, I was walking in a new season of love, celebration, and renewed hope. I had gone from being scorned, derided, and rejected to now being loved, accepted, and celebrated.

I returned home to Lagos, Nigeria, from Jeffrey's medical school graduation and announced to my mother and all my siblings that God had confirmed to me His choice for my husband, that I had accepted Jeffrey's proposal of marriage, and that we both wanted to be married the following year, in the summer of 1988. It would be an understatement to state that my siblings were surprised by my announcement, mainly because they had not seen or met any interested suitors and had no idea that someone was interested in me and wanted to marry me.

Apart from my mother and my sisters, who had seen the numerous cards and letters arriving regularly in the mail and had answered some of the many telephone calls from America that had alerted them to the existence of my persistent American suitor, nobody else knew about him. Even my mother and sisters were still caught off-guard as they did not think that my long-distance relationship with the American was that serious to result in marriage. The fact that, in the beginning, I had assumed his attraction to me was a mere passing fancy that would not last also contributed to the mystery. Also, my erroneous assumption that because he had recently re-dedicated his life to the Lord, he was not spiritually mature enough to be a serious candidate.

When Jeffrey first expressed his interest in me and told me that he was going to marry me, I proceeded to advise him in the spirit of brotherly love that he would be better off keeping his mind and focus on "desiring the sincere milk of the word," so he could grow more mature in the Lord. I had erroneously equated spiritual maturity and the ability to hear from God with the length of time that a person had been saved and supposedly serving the Lord. Therefore, I immediately dismissed his initial professions of love and attraction and explained to him that what he really felt was a Christian and brotherly love. He disagreed, insisting that his love and attraction were definitely not brotherly, Christian love. Then, I had the noble idea to help him by hooking him up with a Christian sister who I felt may be a better fit for him. No wonder he accused me of spiritual arrogance! The other reason I did not take him seriously initially was because I had never imagined, nor had I desired to marry outside of my country or culture. I had always imagined and believed I would marry a Nigerian man, most likely a southern Nigerian man. Also, I fancied that he would be a mature "Bible-thumping, Holy Ghost-filled, born-again brother" who would have been saved much longer than me. I did not take Jeffrey or his advances seriously or consider praying about it until I saw his persistence and unwavering pursuit and interest several months after I had returned home to Lagos, Nigeria.

After my 1985 visit, I felt an unction in my spirit that I should take the matter to the Lord in prayer and not lean on my own understanding. When I prayed about it and laid it before the Lord, I did not get a yes or no answer, but I noticed that my feelings toward him started to change, and I began to think of him with greater fondness. I also began looking forward to his phone calls and letters and praying regularly for him.

As my feelings for him grew, I began to consider that he might be "the one" I had prayed for. The implications of marrying a foreigner and leaving my family and all my friends behind to move to his country began to weigh on my mind. Then, I attended the prophetic conference in Ede, Nigeria, where I addressed my suspicion that maybe this was all part of the enemy's ploy to take me out of God's exciting future plan and sideline me. I thank God for Brother Emeka's wise counsel on the meaning of the prophetic word and his encouragement not to give up on the relationship but to keep praying and seeking God and his guidance. I did not fully comprehend or realize what an amazing miracle God had performed in my life or how exquisitely and masterfully He had orchestrated the events culminating in my relationship with Jeffrey--until I announced to my family that I had accepted his proposal of marriage and that we would like to get married the following year. I could understand why my family felt blindsided by the sudden marriage announcement.

Therefore, I was patient during the process of answering their question about when and how I met him, who he was and what he did, where he was from, who his family was, and all the other details that a concerned family would want to know about any guy who wanted to marry their daughter and sister. In addition, they wanted to know what the implications and the plans for my son were. They were amazed that we had met when I was pregnant, that he had been attracted and interested in me since then, and that not only him but also his family had fully accepted my son.

My friends were even more amazed because not only did I decline their offers to hook me up with eligible prospects, but I had also completely dropped out of the social scene after I became born again. I had routinely declined invitations to dinners and get-togethers and informed my friends that I was waiting on the Lord. One of my friends commented that it seemed I was expecting God to drop the prospects from the sky into my lap while sitting at home. They were concerned that I was taking my fanaticism a bit too far and would probably end up an old maid. Imagine their shock upon hearing that I was getting married to a man none of them knew or had ever heard of, never seen, and did not even know existed.

The biggest shock for me was when I realized that God had started to orchestrate the relationship between Jeffrey and me before I gave my life to Him and became born again, and certainly long before I prayed my impassioned prayer asking God to provide me with the exact husband that Tunde's friend said I could never have.

I met Jeffrey in August 1984 on my first trip to Nashville, TN, while I was eight months pregnant, and he asked me the strange question: Was I going to marry my baby's father? I dismissed his question as nosey and weird and thought nothing more of it; I gave my life to the Lord and was born again on December 5th, 1984, several months after my Nashville trip.

The visit and remarks from Tunde's friend that caused my impassioned prayer occurred in early January 1985. I saw Jeffrey again in July 1985 after attending Kenneth Hagin's Camp Meeting in Tulsa, OK. Shortly after we arrived in town from the airport, he was knocking on the door as if he had been waiting for me to return to Nashville to resume the relationship. Jeffrey stated that he was attracted to me from the first time he met me, even though I was pregnant. He had made up his mind then that if, for any reason, I did not marry the father of my baby, he was going to pursue and marry me!

I was awestruck at the omniscience and loving kindness of this awesome God who had answered and already provided. He answered and already provided for a prayer I had not even known enough to pray at a time when I had not surrendered my life to Him. To take it a step further, during that time, I was blaming Him for my misfortunes as I felt forsaken, abandoned, and unloved! Yet, despite everything I threw at God, I was on His mind.

For me, it truly exemplified His promise in Isaiah 65:24 (KJV), *"Before they call, I will answer; while they are yet speaking, I will hear."* I was beyond ecstatic, and I was glad to share this joy of answered prayers with my family.

CHAPTER THIRTY-NINE

Wedding Preparations & Attacks

In telling them about Jeffrey, I reassured my mother and siblings. I wanted them to know and understand how Jeffrey was a manifestation of an answered prayer. I told them that Jeffrey was a born-again believer who had just graduated from medical school and that he and his family had accepted my son. They were even more excited when I informed them that Jeffrey and his parents, siblings, and other family members were all planning to come to Nigeria to participate in the wedding ceremony.

Finally, the news reassured my mother that Jeffrey's letters addressing me as Mrs. Jola Olufon Moore were not because we had been secretly married but was him exercising his faith, calling those things which be not as though they were, just like I had told her. They were pleased to learn that not only were Jeffrey and his family flying to Lagos to participate in the wedding ceremony, but they had also agreed to take all the steps required by our culture and tradition as part of the wedding ceremony. Now that both families were in agreement with the union, we began to discuss possible dates for the wedding. I requested that Jeffrey ask his parents what month in the year would work best for them to attend the wedding out of deference to their schedule and their budget. He called me, stating that his parents said that it was our wedding, and they did not feel they should impose a date on us and that we should set our wedding on any date we pleased. I asked Jeffrey to explain that we were deferring to them to choose the date out of consideration and understanding that the trip abroad to attend the wedding would involve considerable expense and time for them. However, they still insisted that it was not their place to choose the date.

Therefore, after consulting with my family, we set the wedding for August 1988. A few weeks after setting the date, Jeffrey called to inform me that his parents could not attend the wedding on the date we had set but gave their blessing for us to proceed with the wedding on that date.

My heart sank as I immediately recognized that this was an attack from the enemy. He would not stand by quietly and let me get the wedding of my dreams, with my fiancée's family in attendance and fully participating in every aspect of the wedding ceremony, just like we had all agreed. The enemy wanted to continue his oppression and attack by putting obstacles and barriers in our way.

I realized and discerned that I was in a spiritual warfare, contending with principalities and powers over my marriage and my future. I consecrated myself to a fast and asked my fellow intercessors, brethren of the Prayer Band, to pray and intercede for me. This time around,

I was not unaware of the devices of the enemy, and I knew that the weapons of my warfare were not carnal but mighty through God to the pulling down of strongholds.

At the end of my period of fasting and consecration, I knew in my spirit how to proceed. I telephoned Jeffrey and asked him to inform his parents that the proposed wedding date had been cancelled, and that we would set a new wedding date after they determined when they could attend the wedding. Within two weeks, Jeffrey called me back excitedly to say that his parents had said they could attend the wedding if it was set around Christmas.

We reset the wedding date for Boxing Day, December 26th, 1988, and preparations began in earnest. Jeffrey had informed his family that the first step in the marriage process in the Nigerian Yoruba culture was the letter of introduction and intent, written by the head of the bridegroom's family to the bride's family, officially asking their permission for his son to marry their daughter. This letter is usually printed on fine parchment paper, in gilded print, delivered at an appointed time by representatives of the groom's family. In our case, Jeffrey's father asked my family's indulgence to have the letter delivered by Federal Express as it was being sent from Flint, MI, in the United States. When the letter arrived, my family gathered to open it, prayed over it, and sent a response back to the Moore family in Flint, MI.

The traditional engagement ceremony was scheduled for December 24th, 1988, at my family's home at Lagoon House, Ilaje, Bariga, Nigeria. My future mother-in-law, Dolores Moore, had decided that in accordance with the Yoruba culture for the traditional engagement ceremony, the Moore family delegation would also be dressed in matching traditional Nigerian outfits. So, she had commissioned me to have outfits tailor-made for the Moore family members. We also had a block of rooms reserved for them at the Eko Hotel, Victoria Island, Lagos.

In the late summer of 1988, about four months before the wedding, I flew back to Nashville, TN, to shop for my wedding dress. Mfon had moved back to Maryland to join her sisters after graduation, so, once again, I stayed with Darlene, who was excited and eager to assist me with my wedding shopping. After visiting several stores, we found the wedding dress of my dreams at the Castner Knott department store in downtown Nashville.

I knew that Darlene really wanted to attend the wedding, and I wanted her to be there as well. Jeffrey and I had practically courted in her sitting room, and she had been involved from the inception of the relationship. However, she stated that they could not afford the cost of the ticket to fly to Nigeria, not to mention the cost of the accommodations and other related expenses.

As we shopped together, prepared the wedding announcement, and put together travel cost estimates for Jeffrey's family members to attend the wedding, Darlene sighed and expressed her desire to attend the wedding and be part of it. She said that she had never traveled internationally, out of the United States, and she had always desired to go to Africa. I finally challenged her to make a decision that she would attend the wedding and then trust God to provide the resources.

Darlene agreed. We prayed the prayer of agreement together, and she announced to her husband and children that she had decided to attend Jeffrey and I's wedding in Lagos, Nigeria, and that she was trusting God for the funds to go. Her husband laughed and said it was impossible on their family's current budget and would be a modern-day miracle if it happened. Undaunted, Darlene insisted that she still intended to attend the wedding and trusted God for the funds. I felt God would make provisions for her if she were meant to be part of the special day, so I left it in God's hands.

While I was staying at Darlene's house over that summer of 1988, we attended the Wednesday night Bible study held at the home of one of the other couples, the Blackmans, as the Bible study had grown so big that they needed larger space to meet. At the Bible study at the Blackman home, I first met a fellow African gentleman and his children, who also regularly attended the Bible study. They introduced him as Brother Alex, a professor of political science at Tennessee State University and an avid student of the Bible since getting saved.

I remember getting into a discussion with Brother Alex about a popular book that he had read that had convinced him that the world would come to an end on 8/8/88. He eloquently quoted all the Bible passages and supporting world events that proved the assertions in the book. He was convinced that the prophet who wrote the book was inspired and had done all the necessary research and uncovered all the pertinent evidence to support his assertions.

I stubbornly disagreed and told him that it did not bear witness to my spirit and that God had worked mighty miracles in my life to bring about my wedding to the man of his choice for me. I did not believe that God would have done all He did and got us to set the wedding date for December 26th, 1988, if He intended to bring the world to an end on 8/8/88. I insisted that I believe God's promise to me that my wedding would occur as planned on December 26th, 1988. I had prayed on it and would not allow discouragement no matter what anyone else said. I returned home to Lagos, Nigeria, at the end of July and continued my wedding preparations.

I was very excited and happy when I woke up on the morning of August 9th, 1988, to find that the world had not ended as predicted and that my wedding would occur just as we had planned and God had promised. Miraculously, God began to open several doors of blessings to Darlene and directed people to sow into her life. God fully provided all the resources she needed to travel to Lagos, Nigeria, to attend our wedding. The Lord granted her wish and mine for her to attend the wedding despite the impossible budget scenario.

CHAPTER FORTY

The Wedding

The biggest miracle concerning our wedding, which illustrated and proved to me how much God loved and valued me, was the size of the delegation from the United States of America to participate in our wedding. I was astounded and extremely excited when Jeffrey called me to confirm that ten people altogether had purchased their plane tickets, booked their hotel rooms, and were definitely attending the wedding and also participating in the traditional engagement ceremony, where they would formally come as a family to ask for the bride's hand in marriage and bring gifts for the bride and all her family.

After that phone call, I fell to my knees with tears of joy streaming down my face as I remembered that just four years before, even though I was pregnant with Tunde's child, Tunde's family not only failed to write the letter of intent of marriage, his mother procured a false witness to make accusations against me and not only vehemently opposed the marriage, but also never acknowledged my family. Now, another family of superior pedigree, with a delegation of 10 people, chose to travel halfway around the world to take all the proper steps required of them to ask for my hand in marriage on their son's behalf and to reaffirm what they had earlier stated in their letter to my family; that they lovingly and unconditionally accepted and welcomed both myself and my son into their family.

I loudly praised and thanked my faithful Father and awesome God. I was reminded of Isaiah 62:4 (MSG), *"No more will anyone call you Rejected, and your country will no more be called Ruined. You'll be called Hephzibah (My Delight), and your land Beulah (Married), Because God delights in you and your land will be like a wedding celebration."* I also thought of Psalm 118:22 (MSG), *"The stone the masons discarded as flawed is now the capstone!"* Even though the enemy tried to raise his head a few more times before the wedding day, he had no success. All the intercessors and I had agreed to continue to pray and intercede continuously till the wedding was successfully celebrated. I knew not to leave the enemy any room this time!

One week before the scheduled wedding day, the Moore family delegation arrived safely in Lagos, Nigeria, to a warm welcome and an air-conditioned luxury bus to convey them to their hotel. One of the high points of their visit was the day of the traditional engagement ceremony when they all donned their custom-made African outfits and were escorted by the sisters from the Prayer Band Fellowship; they came singing and bearing gifts to meet my family and formally asked for my hand in marriage.

My wedding day, Saturday, December 26th, 1988, was everything I had dreamed of and a whole lot more. The church was packed to capacity and overflowing with all our family and friends. My oldest brother, who was the head of the family since my father's homegoing years ago, walked me down the aisle of our family church, Olowogbowo Methodist Church, in my gorgeous wedding dress and handed me over to my smiling, excited groom waiting for me at the altar. After the church wedding ceremony, we had a beautiful wedding reception on the grounds of my brother Gbolahan's lovely home on Victoria Island, Lagos.

One of the highlights of the beautiful wedding reception was the custom-made collector porcelain bride and groom dolls that my mother-in-law had flown in from Michigan to be prominently displayed in front of our five-tiered wedding cake on the podium. God had taken me full circle, from a mother who hated and scorned me to a mother who went above and beyond the call of duty to honor me and show me and the whole world how much she loved me. Only God could have accomplished such a feat!

During the reception, when the new bridegroom was handed the microphone to respond to the toast, after thanking God and both families and all our friends for their support, he announced that he would sleep well tonight, as he had waited a long time for this night! As the guests laughed and applauded at his excitement about our wedding night, I blushingly laughed, too, as I silently thanked God for another answered prayer that the man of his choosing would gladly wait until our wedding night to consummate our love.

Later that night, in true Nigerian style, we had a huge soiree, also known as the after-wedding party, complete with a live band and lots of dancing. To my new groom's dismay, he had been sent back to his hotel room by himself after the wedding reception and informed that his bride would be handed over to him and his family at the after-wedding party. At the conclusion of the after-wedding party, the two families were ushered into a private room, where the head of each family, followed by the parents, were asked to pray and lay hands on the newly married couple. Then I was handed over, first to my new parents-in-law and finally to my long-suffering, eager bridegroom!

Our wedding night was beautiful beyond our imagination!

CHAPTER FORTY-ONE

Honeymoon Interrupted

O ur plan was to spend the first part of our
honeymoon at the Eko Hotel in Victoria Island,
Lagos, and then I would leave with the Moore
family delegation, and we would stop in Europe for three
days for the second half of our honeymoon on the way
back to the United States. Since I already had a five-year
multiple entry visa to the United States, we thought that
there was no need for us to visit the American Embassy
in Lagos until Jeffrey's Uncle Herbert, who was also an
attorney, suggested that we pay a visit to the United States
Embassy in Lagos, to ascertain all the documents that I
would need to take with me to adjust my status when I
arrived in the United States.

To our shock and dismay, the consular officer
informed us that I could no longer enter the U.S. on
my multiple-entry visitor's visa. Since I was married
to an American citizen, I was no longer a tourist but a
prospective immigrant. They informed us that if I had
traveled to the U.S. as planned, the immigration officers

at the port of entry would have canceled my visitor's visa and repatriated me back to Nigeria.

They informed us that I had to commence the immigration process in Lagos because we got married there. The process included a complete physical exam with blood work, a background check, fingerprinting, production of numerous records and documents, and an in-person interview at the Embassy, and the process usually took between three months to one year to complete. We were dumbfounded by this information and devastated that our honeymoon was going to be interrupted, and we were going to be separated so soon after our marriage.

Uncle Herb tried very hard to advocate for us, as he questioned the consular officer about any exceptions or loopholes they could apply to us. The officer insisted there was no loophole or exception for entering the U.S. under my current visa. Seeing our crestfallen, mournful countenance, the senior consular officer who interviewed us offered to give us all the necessary forms and do her best to speed up the process on our behalf.

A few days later, I sadly bid my new bridegroom farewell as he returned home without me, feeling like the enemy had sucker-punched me. However, it soon became apparent when I started the immigration process at the American Embassy that what the enemy meant for evil, God had, in fact, permitted to save us from a worse catastrophe later on. If I had left Nigeria after our wedding with the Moores as planned, I would have been repatriated because my tourist visa would have been voided. As a consequence of the repatriation, I would not have been allowed to commence the immigration process for several years. Also, if I had been sent back to Nigeria, it would have made it more difficult for me to apply for my son.

Acting on the counsel of my newfound ally at the American Embassy, we decided to process both my and my son's immigration applications together rather than waiting for one year before applying for him as we had originally intended. The Lord gave me so much favor with the consular officer that she personally expedited our application through the process so fast that the process that would typically take three months to one year was completed within two weeks. My son and I were on the next plane headed to our new home in Nashville, TN.

CHAPTER FORTY-TWO

Rahab & Me

I had my impassioned monologue with God mid-year in 1985, about six to eight months after I was born again. I started attending the weekly Bible study and prayer meeting hosted by the Prayer Band Fellowship Group and found a new joy, hope, and peace, but at the same time, I still felt a lot of shame and guilt about my new status as an unwed mother. As I got a more profound and better understanding of the Word of God, I could see how I had played into the hands of the enemy and set myself up to fail when I made a vow of celibacy instead of yielding my life and my will to God and obeying His word. God had already set parameters in His word for how believers are to live and had given us the Holy Spirit to help us succeed on our journey. Instead, I set up my own terms of obedience and made up the rules along the way.

When the powers of darkness came against me and prevailed against me, I then blamed God for not looking out for me or protecting me. Even though I was now reconciled to God, I still struggled with guilt that I had let my son down by depriving him of the opportunity to have both his parents raise him because of my poor choices.

I did not want any of the young people at the Prayer Band Fellowship to follow in my footsteps or look up to me as a role model. I deliberately always sat in the back and tried my best not to draw any attention to myself. I enjoyed the Bible study and prayer meetings and would leave shortly after it ended. I did not discuss any details about my private life, and l did not socialize much with the other members. Even though I knew that God had forgiven me for my sins when I prayed and asked Him into my heart, I could not forgive myself and felt that I had brought my circumstances upon myself and, therefore, had messed up the bright future I could have had. I felt like "damaged goods," as Tunde's friend had said, a person with limited or second-rate options.

So, when the leaders of the Prayer Band Fellowship informed me that I had been selected to become the Assistant fellowship leader, I was convinced they were mistaken. I felt I was not worthy of a leadership position as I thought that anyone in any Christian leadership position had to be exemplary. They told me to go home, pray about it, and seek the Lord myself, hence my impassioned monologue followed by God's strange answer of, "*If Rahab the Harlot could enter in, so can you.*"

So, why Rahab the Harlot? *What specifically was God pointing me to?* Then it struck me - Rahab had exercised faith! The singular most important element required to please God and receive from him. Hebrews 11:6(NKJV) says, *"But without faith it is impossible to please Him, for he who comes to God must believe that He is, and that He is a rewarder of those who diligently seek Him."* Rahab's words and actions with the spies were proof that she believed in the God of the Jews and that He was a rewarder. Because of Rahab's faith, she and her entire family were the only survivors of the Battle of Jericho. The Israeli spies honored their oath to Rahab, but their God, pleased with her faith, did exceedingly, abundantly above what she could ask or think. He was pointing me to her faith. That still left the other part of God's answer unexplained: *Where did Rahab the Harlot enter into?*

CHAPTER FORTY-THREE

Where Rahab Entered Into

I found the answer in Matthew chapter 1, where Matthew traces the genealogy of Jesus Christ. There, I found, to my amazement, Rahab, the Harlot listed in the genealogy. Matthew 1:5 (NKJV) says, *"Salmon begot Boaz by Rahab."* Wow! Wow! Rahab the Harlot had married into the tribe of Judah, the royal lineage of King David, and the ultimate lineage of Jesus Christ. In other words, Rahab the Harlot had become a great, great, great, great grandmother of Jesus Christ!

Rahab had not only entered the promised land with the Israelites and all her family members, but she had also married into the most exclusive tribe in Israel, the royal lineage of David, that gave us Jesus Christ. How did this woman, whose epithet was "the Harlot," go from being a despised, shunned, looked-down-upon woman of ill repute, a prostitute who exchanged favors for financial gain, make it into the royal lineage of Jesus Christ?

How does Rahab the Harlot become the forebear of Jesus Christ? How did she overcome such insurmountable odds? Particularly in an era when women were regarded as chattel and did not have the right of self-determination. How did she go from the bottom rung of society in an idolatrous and cursed nation to marrying into one of the leading families in Israel? How did a heathen harlot enter into the royal lineage?

It was certainly not through the benevolence or promotion of men. The stigma of who Rahab used to be and what she used to do would have certainly excluded her from the elite society in Israel. However, her strong admiration for and total trust in the God of Israel, without the benefit of any prior personal experience, must have made a big impression on the two Israeli spies.

Salmon, one of the spies, was so struck by this most unusual heathen harlot and could discern that there was a lot more to this woman than her derogatory title would suggest. He could tell that Rahab was a diamond in the rough, and his gratitude for her action in saving his and his friend's lives must have grown into admiration and morphed into love. His love would have had to be very strong and enduring enough to withstand and prevail against the outcry and opposition of his elite, upper-class family and tribesmen, their horror at his decision to marry a former heathen harlot and make her a member of their tribe. Of all the chaste and pure Israeli women of class and breeding that Salmon could have chosen, he chose to marry Rahab the Harlot.

How did Rahab, the heathen harlot, become Rahab, the ancestress of Jesus Christ? By first becoming an admirer and then a lover of the God of Israel. After hearing all the stories of the exploits that the God of Israel had performed on behalf of his people, she became an admirer. Her admiration grew so much that she must have wished in her heart that she could belong to and serve such an awesome God, the God who knows the hearts of men arranged for her to have the opportunity to prove herself.

Since her heart was prepared and she was already a secret admirer of the God of Israel, the minute Rahab laid eyes on the Israeli spies and recognized who they were, she sprang into action to show her allegiance to this great God of Israel of whom she declared to the two spies in Joshua 2:11 (NKJV), *"the Lord your God, He is God in heaven above and in earth beneath."* Rahab's attention right from the onset was on the God of Israel and her transactions and requests were directed to Him through the Israeli spies. According to Rahab, all the inhabitants of Jericho had heard of the exploits performed by the God of Israel and were in terror of the Israelites, and she had chosen to change allegiance and put her faith in their God.

Rahab proved her faith by her brave action of risking her own life to save the lives of the spies, without them asking her to do so and without her making any demand of them. Her thoughts were centered solely on the God of Israel, whom she had trusted and honored and who had promoted and justified her by her works.

Ye see then how that by works a man is justified, and not by faith only. Likewise also was not Rahab the harlot justified by works, when she had received the messengers, and had sent them out another way? For as the body without the spirit is dead, so faith without works is dead also.

JAMES 2:24-26 (KJV)

For context, James mentioned in this chapter how Abraham was justified by his works when he offered up Isaac. James then concludes the chapter by comparing Rahab the Harlot to Abraham, the father of faith!

As if that high honor was not enough, the Lord showed me where else Rahab the Harlot had entered into. Rahab had also entered into the ultimate Hall of Fame recorded in Hebrew:11, that illustrious roll of the Old Testament Saints who had triumphed by faith. In Hebrews 11:31 (KJV), the Bible says, *"By faith the harlot Rahab perished not with them that believed not, when she had received the spies with peace."* Rahab the Harlot is listed along with Abraham, Moses, Jacob, and Sarah and is the only other woman listed in this Hall of Fame.

What a manifestation of the mercy, love, and sovereignty of this incredible God, who would rank a former heathen harlot worthy of equal honor as the patriarchs and fathers of the faith like Abraham, Moses, David, and the prophet Samuel.

Epilogue

So, now, I know where Rahab the Harlot had entered into. Now, I understand the answer God had given to my impassioned monologue. Now that I know who this mighty woman of God really is, I am in awe and feel so humbled that God would compare me to her.

I believe that I now comprehend the complete message of what the Lord was saying to me: *"If Rahab the Harlot could enter into the genealogy of Jesus Christ, so can you!"* If a one-time heathen harlot could overcome her past and rise from the dunghill, press in to enter into the most exclusive genealogy, and become a forebear and ancestress of Jesus Christ, her past definitely did not determine her future! If she could enter into the most exclusive Hall of Fame in the Bible, I could surely overcome the shame, guilt, and embarrassment of being an unwed mother and courageously move forward in my faith to accomplish my destiny in Jesus.

Surely, I can come out of hiding, stop being concerned about what people might think of my past, and press forward to embrace God's bright future for me. Surely, I could humbly and gratefully accept and embrace my new office and calling as the assistant leader of the Prayer Band and trust God to use me as He saw fit. Surely, I could entrust my future and my son's future into the hands of the same great God, who not only saved Rahab the Harlot's life but catapulted her into the royal lineage of David and Jesus because she loved and believed in Him.

I could gladly entrust my life and all my hopes and dreams to this kind of God without giving a second thought to the inconsequential opinions of mere men.

AFTERWORD

40 Years Later

This year, 2024, marks the 40th anniversary of:

- Meeting my Yankee Doodle, Jeffrey, who was attracted to me from the start, even though I was pregnant, and said he knew in his heart that he would marry me. We celebrate our 36th wedding anniversary this year!

- The birth of my firstborn son, who the Lord told me would be a blessing and a leader among men.

- The surrender of my life to Jesus and becoming born again.

The Lord impressed on my heart that I needed to complete and publish this book this year, the 40th anniversary of the sequence of events that started with me getting pregnant, the relationship ending, meeting the man whom God (unbeknown to me) had chosen and prepared to love and cherish my son and me, the birth of my amazing son, and finally, my heart and mind becoming unshackled, when I invited Jesus into my life and became born again. I look forward to many more years walking with Him and fulfilling the glorious destiny He has ordained for me as I keep falling in love with Him, over and over and over and over again!

I pray that you also experience the unspeakable joy filled with glory that only comes from knowing Him.

LAST WORD

If Rahab the Harlot, who without pedigree or breeding and without coach or mentor, could enter by faith into the lineage of God Himself, so can you.

Acknowledgments

I want to acknowledge and thank the following people. First, my Yankee-Doodle, my amazing husband, greatest cheerleader and best friend. You have always loved me with a tenderness and care that models the love of God to me. I am eternally grateful that God hand-picked you, specifically for me, you have been all that I asked for and so much more. Thank you for all your technical support and continuous encouragement, without which this project would have not been possible.

I want to thank my guys, Siji, Jeffrey Jr, and Joshua and our Princess Mayo of Goodlettsville, for your love and the joy that you each add to my life, I count it a privilege and an anointed calling to be your mother and chief intercessor. Excited at the amazing things God is doing and will yet do in each of your lives.

I want to thank all my siblings in Nigeria and London for their enduring love and support all my life and particularly during the fragile and turbulent times, when their love and support was crucial. I thank God for my wonderful siblings. I want to acknowledge and thank my friend Darlene, for allowing the Lord to use her to support and nurture Jeff and

I at the beginning of our relationship and for attending our wedding in Lagos, Nigeria and proposing the toast.

I want to acknowledge and thank my friend Mfon, for her love and support all through the years and being the one God used to bring Jeff and I together.

I want to acknowledge and thank Pastor Alexander Arthur, our Pastor for thirty three years at Word of Life Christian Center International, for his love and support, his teaching and nurturing, and for being one of the first persons to confirm to me, by prophecy, that the Lord was calling me to share my salvation testimony and to write a book.

At a time when the writing process seemed to stall and I felt stuck and unable to move forward, the Lord used Patricia to connect me to Latoya, who was like a breath of fresh air and helped me formulate the vision for the cover and connected me with a publisher, who had the experience and capability to help me publish my book within the time frame I had received from the Lord. Thank you Patricia and Latoya, I am truly grateful for your help and counsel.

Last but not least, I want to thank Gabriela, who works with us as our Assistant Office Manager, for designing the book cover after I shared my vision and Latoya's inspired suggestion to have the scarlet cord run through the calligraphy, she came up with the lovely design for the cover. Thank you also Gabby for volunteering to take my head shots, thank you for sharing your gifts and talents, so generously.

Thank you to all my reviewers for agreeing to review my book with such short notice and over a holiday period! Thank you for your love and support and kindness.

Blessings & Love

About the Author

Jola Moore was licensed as an attorney in Nigeria in 1981 and in Tennessee in 1989 and continues to enjoy the practice of law. After giving her life to Jesus, and due to the traumatic events in her life that led her to salvation, and thereafter marrying her husband, she developed a new passion to see young ladies choose their life partners in accordance with God's guidance and direction, also a passion to help marriages endure and thrive.

Jola developed a passionate love for God as a result of His amazing intervention in her life and the manner in which He provided the partner of His choosing for her before she knew to ask him.

Jeff and Jola have been married for 36 years and are the blessed parents of four adult children, Babasijibomi (Amanda), Jeffrey Jr. (Ashley), Joshua, and Mayomikun. They have three wonderful grandchildren, Olumide Amaka, Asiwaju, and Amara.

www.ingramcontent.com/pod-product-compliance
Lightning Source LLC
Chambersburg PA
CBHW020409150626
46554CB00012B/421